Wake up!
if you can

Other translations by Anthea Guinness

The inner way: A mystic anthology of songpoems, stories, reflections SUITABLE FOR AGE 13 ON UP

Soami Ji of Agra answering questions: Mystic teachings on the path of inner sound, 2 *volumes*

POCKETBOOK *Dawn has come: Songpoems of Paltu*

Wake up!
if you can

sayings of Kabir
with reflections
and mystic stories

translated by Anthea Guinness

 SALT RIVER

GLOBAL LIBRARY

is an imprint of Salt River Publishing
Phoenix, Arizona
www.SaltRiverPublishing.com

SECOND EDITION 2015
19 18 17   7 6 5   IV III II
ISBN 978-1-5194132-8-4

Library of Congress Control Number: 2015919338

Cover photo by Greg Meyer (*see Colophon*), used with permission: Indian scops owl, Ranthambore National Park, Rajasthan, India

Publisher discount available
SaltRiverPublishing.com/estore/

CONTENTS

special sayings addressed to issues and challenges they personally were facing… in the way masters sometimes do today?

However the sayings came about, one can imagine Kabir's disciples were reminded of their master every time they recited them — reminded of his love, his smile, his attention, the radiance of his eyes, the tranquil atmosphere of his presence. And his teachings.

This fund of practical reminders is a wonderful resource for seekers and meditators, whatever one's background or particular spiritual practice may be.

The charm of the *dohas* lies in the way Kabir words his advice — through a vivid image, his quick wit or the unexpected turn he gives to a line. And the lightness and brilliance of these little gems may even disguise, at first, the depth of their spiritual meaning.

Pithy and conversational, the tone of the sayings and Kabir's obvious intelligence, humour and understanding open the heart, make one smile — and bring about a willingness to pay attention for a moment to his message. His purpose? To challenge the seeker within us to think more deeply and to inspire us to action.

> Like oil in sesame seeds,
> fire in flint stone,
> your Beloved is inside you.
> If you can, wake up –
> really wake up![2]

"Really waking up" involves a total transformation of consciousness – an inward focusing in meditation that may take decades to develop, or that may be immediate, depending on one's spiritual state and prior experience.

Kabir's "wake up" saying suggests it takes hard work, persistence and a well-tried method to become aware of anything inside. His audience in the 1400s would appreciate that manually kindling fire or extracting oil require knowledge and skill in addition to dedicated action – patient, persevering, focused… as does spiritual practice.

Most of his listeners were probably oblivious, as many of us are, to their own extraordinary potential – unaware or uncertain whether there is such a thing as an on-going inner reality that we are capable of experiencing.

Who would think of fire when looking at a piece of flint stone? Who sees a bottle of oil when looking at a bag of sesame seeds?

Kabir's imagery is vivid: if somebody wants to manifest whatever is hidden behind the mask of their physical body and mind, they need to learn how to kindle the "fire" of inner light and extract the "oil" or divine essence. Emphasizing the value of that mysterious spiritual essence, Kabir says in another *doha*:

> Money cannot buy the word –
> if you know how to say that word.
> You can price a diamond
> but how can you weigh
> the voicing of the word![3]

Knowledge of inner mysteries is recorded in gnostic and sacred writings in every culture and spiritual tradition. It is called word (shabd, kalma, logos), the essence, the thing, the light, name, spirit, secret, tao, voice, sound or music, among many other terms.

The paradox is that we refer to it as the word, the name, the voice, but according to the mystics none of us can "say" that word or name, nor can we weigh, measure or record its sound, its voice. And that "voicing" of the word, says Kabir, is so precious it is beyond price. In another *doha* he explains why:

> There are millions of names in the world
> but none of them leads to liberation.
> If you meditate on the primal name

in secret, you might be among the few
who realize it.[4]

Shabd or naam is priceless because it has the power
to uplift and free the individual's consciousness from all
the limitations that hold it tied down to the body and
mind. Once liberated, our consciousness is free in this
life to evolve towards its full potential, its natural or true
state, characterized by love, tranquillity and bliss:

> Where the shabd rings out
> with loud beating of drums
> and twanging strings, within –
> in adoration I touched its light
> and found my master.
>
> Says Kabir, this game
> is played by mendicants.
> Playing well, they reach home
> and their true state –
> with ease![5]

Kabir most often calls the inner power *shabd* (word,
sound) or *naam* (name) – sometimes just "the thing".

Love-intoxicated mystics who know how to play the game of life are "mendicants", travelling through the inner worlds to reach the soul's true home. And like other bhakti mystics before and since, Kabir associates the game with inner light, inner sound, the inner form of the master, and the return journey to our spiritual source.

Kabir frequently speaks of the inner path as *surat shabd,* meaning the attuning and merging of our individual consciousness (surat) in universal consciousness (shabd):

> My master is in the skies,
> disciple in his heart.
> Once surat has merged in shabd,
> there's no separation
> ever again.[6]

How does one set about evolving spiritually? However deeply we may desire or believe, Kabir says we cannot achieve spiritual transformation through our own unaided efforts. That is why he ends the earlier *doha* by challenging us to wake up "if you can" – implying that the task is impossible… on our own.

From their own experience, the mystics know the inner journey is immense and the path so subtle that one needs the help of an expert – a guide.

Bhakti mystics like Kabir define the guide as a practitioner of shabd who teaches shabd. Their consciousness has merged in shabd and their mission is to link their disciples with shabd. Even the master's body is projected from shabd – or as some mystics put it, the master is shabd incarnate, the "word made flesh".[7]

> The master and the Lord are one –
> twoness is just an appearance.
>
> Erase your ego
> through devotion to the master –
> only then can you attain the Creator![8]

Kabir indicates that the task of the "complete teacher" (*pooran satguru* or *murshid-i kaamil*) is to teach seekers about their spiritual potential – and help them realize it.

> If God and guru
> were both standing here,
> at whose feet would I bow?
>
> I'd throw myself at the feet
> of my master – he told me
> all about God![9]

Ultimately, what is it that brings about a person's awakening? Pure grace! Or as Kabir puts it:

> First the Giver becomes a disciple
> who offers up body and mind –
> even his head.

> Then the Giver becomes the guru
> who showers the blessing
> of the name.[10]

The mystics even say effort in meditation has just one purpose: to become receptive to grace. For most people, receptivity develops slowly because it requires one-pointed attention. The meditation practice itself shows the disciple how difficult it is to control body and mind, to focus and hold the attention – and how essential to become receptive to inner assistance from the master.

Failing to sit still and hold the attention inside is humbling for the ego, no doubt – especially if it goes on for years or even decades. But it is worthwhile if it keeps leading to more effort.

For hundreds of years the mystics have repeatedly encouraged their disciples to go on with their spiritual practice, to keep "ruminating" – with the assurance that there are no failures, just a bit more effort is needed.

How can they be sure? Because the master himself is the embodiment of shabd and he knows it is by his grace and power that the goal of realization will be reached.

And what is that power and grace? The bhakti mystics say it is love. They say the master repays the disciple's efforts with the wages of love. In his own time and at a pace the disciple can handle, the master awakens his disciples to the invisible: the all-consuming presence of divine love within – hidden "like oil in sesame seeds, fire in flint stone".

> My Beloved is inside every body –
> not a wedding bed without him!
>
> But I would give my life to those
> with their bodies of clay
> when he has manifested
>
> inside them.[11]

For the bhakti disciple, that manifesting within of the master in his shabd or radiant form – brilliant with light, resounding with a music indescribably beautiful – is when the journey really begins: the extraordinary evolution, through love, towards truth, oneness and spiritual union, while one is alive.

Kabir's sayings sparkle! They feel simple, down-to-earth and enjoyable – but there is a sense that most of them are packed with meaning, asking to be unrolled, shaken out and looked at in detail.

The reflections in the following pages are personal unravellings of Kabir's sayings interspersed with comments on mystic meanings. The notes minimize information on Kabir's naam bhakti teachings given here in the introduction and they do not define frequently used terms like consciousness, Beloved or simran, because they are discussed in the Glossary.

As for the stories in this book – the mystics have often told stories, to illustrate points, catch our attention, help us relax, encourage us to open up or laugh…

Mystics don't limit themselves to stories belonging to any particular spiritual tradition – they use anything that conveys a truth, regardless of its source or style. Contemporary mystics draw on multiple sources, from risqué wedding jokes to the *Reader's Digest*. Shams of Tabriz in the 1100s sometimes tells bawdy stories or uses images that some editors consider crude, too earthy.[12]

And what about Kabir?

We have no idea whether Kabir told stories or what they might have been. The mystic stories interwoven here are modern retellings of traditional stories that represent a range of backgrounds, styles and moods. They affirm the message of Kabir's poems – and much as though Kabir himself were the storyteller, they make us smile or touch the heart as his message goes home.

The intention of *Wake up! if you can* is to offer – thanks to Kabir – a homeopathic dose of hope, help and humour for the way. The mystic sayings and stories remind us, as a contemporary mystic once said, that the path is more long than hard. And as Kabir tells us: Bring the master along with you – then this path that should take a million lifetimes will take no time at all![13]

> Kabir, when my mind became as pure
> as the sacred waters of the Ganga,
> God himself began roaming round
> after me, calling "Kabir, Kabir!"[14]

101

sayings
of
Kabir

with reflections
and mystic stories

The way of bhakti, devotion,
begins with love –

the magnetic pull of the master's
unconditional love.

Seekers respond to that love…
feel drawn to the master,
interested in his teachings.

Ultimately, when love takes over,
the master becomes visible
inside. That

is pure joy!

HINDI SAYING, PRÉM SECTION
prém chhipaaya na chhipai, ja ghaт pargaт hoé;
jo pai mukh bolai nahee~, to nain dét hai~ roé.

1

*H*ow do you propose to hide love!
When it manifests inside
there's no hiding it.

You may hold back from talking
but your eyes, your tears,
will give you away.

What happens when love takes over?
Mind is emptied
of everything

but the Beloved.
No separate identity –

just oneness
in God.

HINDI SAYING, LAV SECTION
sovau~ to supné milai, jaagau~ to man maahi~;
loyan raata sudhi hari, bichhurat kabahu~ naahi~.

2

If asleep, you dream of him.
If awake, he's in your mind.

Eyes so immersed
you're conscious only of God –

never separate
even for a moment.

*L*ove is something
you have to experience –
no words.

And when you have a taste of it?
All you can do is murmur –

incomprehensible…

and smile!

HINDI — KG PAD 156, TÉK
akath kahaaɴi prém ki, kachhu kaihee na jaaee;
goongé kéri sarkara, baiᴛʜé musukaaee.

3

It cannot be told,
the tale of love –
what can you say!

Mute, tongue-tied:
eats the sweets
but where are the words?

Just sits there.
Smiling.

It may be years
  before a disciple is ready

for the bliss of seeing
the shabd master
inside.

Meanwhile, there's the fragrance –

his compassion, kindness, forgiveness...

his look, his walk, his laughter...

meditation –
that, too: fragrance.

HINDI SAYING, SATSANG SECTION
kabeer sangat saadh ki, jyo~ gandhi ka baas;
jo gandhi kachhu déi nahee~, tau bhee baas subaas.[1]

4

*T*he company of a saint?
Like a perfumer's.

He may not give you
any perfume, Kabir

but you'll smell
that fragrance!

What prevents us
from seeing the master
inside?

Lack of love
and a mountain
of karmic interactions.

All of that is destroyed
instantly

in the love fire of naam.

HINDI SAYING, NAAM SECTION
jabahi~ naam hirdé dhara, bhaya paap ka naas;
maano chingi aag ki, pari puraani ghaas.[2]

5

The moment naam
seizes your heart,
all your debts – destroyed.

Ever seen dry grass in flames
from just one spark?

Like that.

The master guarantees
his disciples' karmic debts
will be paid:

he stands as ransom.

And the disciple's role?
To use simran
and climb the ladder –

listening to the inner sound.

HINDI – KG PAD 108, *MAN RÉ KAAGAD KEER PARAAYA*
gurudév gyaani bhayau laganiyaa~, sumiran deenhau
heera; baRi nisarana naa~o raa~m kau, chaDhi gayau
keer kabeera.

6

My beloved master
in his wisdom paid the charge –
and gave me the diamond
of simran.

This name of God,
it's one great big ladder.
The worm Kabir
has climbed right
to the
top!

*L*eft to the law of justice
the path would be millions of lives long

because of our unpaid karmic debts.

But the thing, shabd,
takes you
to complete freedom.

Beyond karma, beyond time.

HINDI SAYING, GURUDÉV SECTION
bhédi leenha saath kar, deenhee bastu lakhaaé;
koti janam ka panth tha, pal mé~ pahu~cha jaaé.[3]

7

When you take
the diviner along,
he shows you the thing.

It's a million lives long, this path –
but you get there
in no time!

It's ego that haggles,
arguing for a point
in the arena of spirituality.

This life is a chance
to do the practice
given by the "seller" of love – the satguru.

The Beloved
is worth sacrificing
everything for –

even thoughts,
identity.

HINDI SAYING, PRÉM SECTION
prém bikanta mai~ suna, maatha saaté haaт;
boojhat bilamb na keejiyé, tatchhin deejai kaaт.

8

*G*uess what – love is on sale!
Where?
In the market.
How much?
Your head.

Don't waste time haggling –
cut off your head and hand it over!

This lifetime is precious.

We can throw it away
like a plucked leaf

or use it to realize our oneness,
our profound connection

with the tree of the divine.

HINDI SAYING, CHITAAVANI SECTION
manush janam durlabh ahai, hoé na baarambaar;
tarvar sé patta jharai, bahuri na laagai DAAR.[4]

9

*T*his human birth –
not so easy to get. You think
it's automatic each time!

When a leaf separates
from the tree, you can't force it
to join again.

Why should we sacrifice
our sleep?
To see what?

Kabir says: To be with the Beloved –

in meditation
with him.

HINDI SAYING, NIDRA SECTION
kabeer soya kya karai, kaahé na dékhai jaagi;
ja ké sang té~ beechhura, tahee ké sang laagi.[5]

10

Kabir, what's the point
of sleeping – why not
stay awake and see?

Absorb yourself
in his company –

you've been separated
so long...

$\mathcal{T}$ranquillity
is an extraordinary state:

stillness

so profound
that even the soul's
hearing and seeing are stilled.

How to achieve that stillness?

He doesn't tell us
here.

HINDI SAYING, SUMIRAN SECTION
tan thir man thir bachan thir, surat nirat thir hoé;
kaih kabeer is palak ko, kalap na paavai koé.[6]

11

*B*ody still.
Mind still.
Words still.
Soul's hearing and seeing:
still.

Says Kabir, in a trillion lifetimes
you won't get a moment
like that!

The camel – it's anything
the master tells us to do
that we find challenging:

some of us give up in frustration,
some of us argue, analyse and question,
some of us go into action.

The point is to please the master
by trying to do
what he says.

And in spite of everything
to keep on
trying.

EN[7]

*Once upon a time, a rich man
said to his servants, "Take a camel
onto the roof" – and then left.*

*The servants gape at one another.
One says, "That's impossible! How
can we get a camel up the stairs?"
Another says, "I wonder why he
wants a camel on the roof?"*

*A third servant runs for the door.
"Where are you off to?" they shout.
"I'm going to get a camel. He said
to take a camel onto the roof – so
I'm taking it onto the roof."*

Whatever we are doing,
it's all the mind.

Our choice,
where we focus
our attention –

inward,
outward.

HINDI SAYING
kabeer man to ék hai, bhaavé tahaa~ lagaaé;
bhaavé guru ki bhakti kar, bhaavé vishay kamaaé.

12

$\mathcal{K}$abir, it's the same one mind
wherever you focus it –

whether you devote yourself
to the practice of the master

or to everything
you lust for.

$\mathcal{T}$he outward way,
the inward way…

Kabir throws a curve ball:
Think! Who and what

do you want to give
your heart to?

HINDI SAYING[8]
kaami ka gur kaamini, lobhi ka gur daam;
kabeer ka gur sant hai, santan ka gur naam.

13

Guru for a guy in love –
his girl.

Guru for the greedy –
money.

Guru for Kabir –
the saint.

Guru for the saints?
Naam.

*W*e all know
what it's like to be in love.

Kabir invites us
to turn that capacity
inward –

become a lover obsessed
with the Beloved

thinking of him
all the time

through simran.

HINDI SAYING, SUMIRAN SECTION
sumiran ki sudhi yo~ karau, jaisé kaami kaam;
ék palak bisarai nahee~, nisu din aaтнo~ jaam.

14

*D*o the practice of simran
like this: Repeating,
remembering, like a lover
obsessed with desire.

Lovers don't forget
even for a second –
day, night,
twenty-four hours.

*G*oing inside
is as simple as closing your eyes?

For most disciples,
easier said than done:

Attention
in simran...

the outlets
for mind and senses
close –

the inner door
opens.

HINDI SAYING, SUMIRAN SECTION
*sumiran surati lagaa'i ké, mukh té~ kachhoo na bol;
baahar ké paт déi ké, antar ké paт khol.*

15

*I*t's your attention
that does simran –
your tongue says nothing at all.

Close the shutters out here –
open up the ones
inside!

$\mathcal{K}$abir says
be quiet, be still:

absorb your mind fully
in that repetition –
inside.

Unexpected results!

HINDI SAYING, SUMIRAN SECTION
maalaa phérat man khusi, ta té~ kachhoo na hoé;
man maalaa ké phératé, ghaт ujiyaaraa hoé.[9]

16

*U*sing a rosary
pleases the mind no end –
but what's the point?
You won't get anything from it.

See what happens when you turn
your mind into a rosary:

Ahh –
your whole body
blazes with light!

$\mathcal{Y}$ou do simran
when you are happy
because you are absorbed

in the Beloved.

That
is what keeps
the attention high

above the intensity
of passing unhappiness.

HINDI SAYING, SUMIRAN SECTION
dukh mé~ sumiran sab karai, sukh mé~ karai na koé;
jo sukh mé~ sumiran karai, to dukh kaahé hoé.[10]

17

*E*verybody does simran
when they're suffering –
nobody does it
when they're happy.

If you do simran
when you're happy,
how can you be unhappy
ever again!

*S*imran lifts your attention

to where the radiant form
of the shabd master appears
inside.

Oneness in shabd –

nothing
more blissful
than that.

HINDI SAYING, SUMIRAN SECTION
sumiran sé sukh hot hai, sumiran sé dukh jaaé;
kaih kabeer sumiran kiyé, saaee maahi~ samaaé.

18

What comes from simran?
Happiness...
Pain and suffering go away...

How?
Through simran, Kabir,
you merge in the Beloved!

$\mathcal{T}$he shabd melody
is deep inside all of us —

inside the clay pot
of this body.

Shabd is the essence
of our consciousness —
who we are.

We don't reach it
through words.

HINDI SAYING, SUMIRAN SECTION
saihaijé hee dhun hot hai, har dam ghaт ké maahi~;
surat sabad méla bhaya, mukh ki haajat naahi~.[11]

19

*T*he sound comes
all by itself: deep inside
this clay pot of yours.

When your consciousness
merges with shabd,
it's no thanks to your mouth!

Shabd is subtle
not physical.

It permeates everything.

Why listen to it?
It's a question of

freedom
from transmigration.

And joy!

kabeer sabad sareer mé~, bin gun baajai taant;
baahar bheetar rami raha, taa té~ chhooᴛee bhraanti.[12]

20

*K*abir, the sound
is inside your body.
Music plays – no strings
anywhere.

Outside, inside –
it's everywhere!

Listen to it and you'll be free
from this whirling around,
death to rebirth.

*S*poken and written words
are different from
the inner word.

It's easy to get caught up
in outer sounds
and beautiful words.

But there is just one sound,
one word, we need. And

a master of it.

HINDI SAYING, SHABD SECTION
sabad sabad bahu antara, sabad saar ka seer;
sabad sabad ka khojana, sabad sabad ka peer.[13]

21

*H*uge difference
between sound-word
and sounds, words.

Shabd is the essence:
reality manifest.

That is the sound
(the sound of sounds!)
you need to search for –
a master
of that word of words.

🌺

$\mathcal{T}$he essence word –
that inner power –
is what merges us in reality.

But there's harvesting to do:

holding on to the inner sound,
letting go of the rest – the chaff.

HINDI SAYING, SHABD SECTION
sabad sabad bahu antara, saar sabad chit déi;
ja sabadai saahib milai, soee sabad gahi léi.[14]

22

*Y*es, a huge difference
between word and words.
Focus on the essence word,
the sound of reality.

The word that will take you
and merge you in the Lord –
that's the one to harvest:
thresh it, gather it up!

To go where the mystics live
we need to
unburden ourselves

of expectations and concepts:
all that thinking
we are so proud of.

But we want proof
of the inner reality...
Kabir says: Sure –

if you can fly!

HINDI SAYING, SOOKSHAM MAARG SECTION
kabeer ka ghar sikhar par, jahaa~ silhili gail;
paa~o na ʈikai papeeli ka, panɒit laadai bail.[15]

23

*K*abir's home
is at the summit.
The way there –
slippery, my friend.

No hold
even for an ant's foot –
but scholars try,
loaded like a bullock!

Sometimes the mystics shock us –

to make a point,
to make us think,
to confuse us.

This story is one of those times.

The disciple is the complacent housewife,
feeding the occasional charity
when it comes knocking at our door

and feeling spiritually satisfied
in general

and with our generosity
in particular.

There was once a Sufi ascetic who used to make the rounds of the town at lunchtime, begging for food.

One day, after a housewife has filled his bowl, he turns to go. "No blessing, no words of guidance? What sort of holy man are you!" she calls after him.

He glances back. "You want to know? I'll come tomorrow at the same hour."

The mystics know we are asleep –
but ready, perhaps,
to wake up.

Meanwhile, we are full of
expectations. We feel we have
earned something special.

And we are right –
but it doesn't come
in the way we expect.

The next morning very early
the housewife begins preparing
an array of delicious foods,
looking forward to the blessing
she will receive and the holy man's
words of wisdom.

Finally lunchtime arrives. The
mendicant enters her courtyard
carrying a plate. She hurries out
with a tray of dishes to serve him,
greeting him respectfully.

Without a word, he holds out
the plate. It is covered in feces.

She steps back, horrified.

Reality check.

Pause.

More inner work to be done!

*She: "What do you mean by this?
I have spent hours preparing
delicious food for you. How can I
put it in a filthy plate like that?"*

*He: "I have spent decades, life-
times, on the path towards
realization. How can I put words
of wisdom into a mind like yours
that is filthy with the world?"*

*She looks down, confused. When
she looks up again, he has gone.*

Paradox: the word has
no form, no physical shape

yet needs to be found
through and in a living form –

the body.

HINDI SAYING, SHABD SECTION
sabad sabad sab koé kaihai, vo to sabad bidéh;
jibhya par aavai nahee~, nirakhi parakhi kari déh.

24

*W*ord, Word –
everybody talks about it

but that word has no
body, shape or form. Nor
can your tongue say it
or sound it.

You want to see it and prove it?
Do it –
through your body!

$\mathcal{T}$he downward pull
of body, mind and the world
is tremendous.

So is the heavy weight
of unpaid karmic debts.

For Kabir
the only counter-pull
is shabd.

HINDI SAYING, SHABD SECTION
*yahi baʀaa'i sabad ki, jaisé chumbak bhaaé;
bina sabad nahi~ oobarai, kéta karai upaaé.*[16]

25

*H*ere's what is great
about the sound:
it attracts like a magnet.

Without that pull of shabd
soul is not liberated –

it doesn't matter
how many methods
you master.

What is the secret of shabd?

Shabd reveals itself
bit by bit.

And the only way
to experience any of it

is to merge into it,
become one with it.

HINDI SAYING, SHABD SECTION
sabad bhéd tab jaaniyé, raihai sabad ké maahi~;
sabadai sabad pragaт bhayaa, dooja deekhai naahi~.

26

*T*he secret of shabd?
You'll only know it
when you remain
inside it.

Shabd manifests
through shabd –
one revealing the next.

No other way
to see it.

$\mathcal{W}$e are naturally
earnest when we begin
something new –

especially
when it involves
spirituality…

A teacher was invited to give
instruction to a group of seekers.

He talks about striving to be free
from strong reactions in daily
life… developing a compassionate
lifestyle… and giving regular time
to a meditation practice he
explains in detail.

The idea is to realize the one divine
life pervading all things.

He concludes: "In the end
you must come to this realization

How
to hold on to spiritual truth
all day long?

What to do
about that old frustration
of a leaky mind?

not just in the meditation period
but in daily life. The whole process
is like filling a sieve with water."

He bows and leaves.

The disciples are puzzled. Some
are frustrated. They know exactly
what it feels like to be a sieve,
leaking out good intentions
and living empty…

Is the master saying
realization is impossible?

We do our best –
and we end up a little wet,
but we can't hold on

to even a cupful
of awareness.

Eventually
we give up, confused –

empty, open…

And that's when the master
sinks the self
in the sea!

EN[17]

In their next meeting, somebody
asks the meaning of the sieve.
The master tells them to bring
a sieve and takes them down
the road to the seashore.

"Show me how you fill the sieve."

One by one they dip it into
the waves and hold it up
while the water rushes out.

"Right, that's one way to do it.
And then there's this way" – and
he hurls the sieve out to sea,
beyond the waves, where it fills
with water and sinks.

$\mathcal{W}$atershed moment
on the journey towards realization:

individual mind
merges back
into the sky of its origins.

Soul is no longer
weighed down
by mind, karma, transmigration.

Freedom!
Finally –
on the way home.

HINDI SAYING, SHABD SECTION
*man taha~ gagan samaaé, dhuni suni suni kai magan
hvai; nahi~ aavai nahi~ jaaé, sunn sabad thiti
paavahee.*[18]

27

*W*here mind merges
in the sky of mind –

listening again and again
to the music,
those melodies –
absorbed, in love:

no more coming, no going.
Instead – pure sound
devoid of mind.

For Kabir, the light
of millions of suns and moons
is darkness.

Light

is when you find
the true master.

HINDI SAYING, GURUDÉV SECTION
koᴛin chanda oogavé~, sooraj koᴛi ujaar;
satguru miliya baaharé, deesat ghor andhaar.[19]

28

*I*f a million moons
were to rise
and millions of suns
lit the sky –

what you'll see
is darkness

unless you have found
the satguru.

Joy and gratitude to the master
for guiding the disciple
to realization –

through complete surrender,
letting go of self.

The mystics say
the realization process
may take years

but the actual transformation
takes a moment.

HINDI SAYING, GURUDÉV SECTION
balihaari guru aapané, ghaʀi ghaʀi sau sau baar;
maanush sé dévta kiya, karat na laagi baar.

29

*E*verything that's me –
body, mind, life – I'd sacrifice
to my master. Not once:
hundreds of times every hour!

He turned me
from human
into God –
and took no time to do so.

Visiting your auntie's home
in Indian and Pakistani families,
you are spoilt, cosseted, indulged.

Kabir gives a reality check:
Don't think the path
is fun and games.

Going inside and evolving
towards full realization,
the home of love, requires

surrendering the ego –
a challenging process
at the best of times.

HINDI SAYING, PRÉM SECTION
yaha to ghar hai prém ka, khaala ka ghar naahi~;
sees utaarai bhu'i~ dharai, tab paiᴛhai ghar maahi~.

30

This is the home of love
we're talking about,
not a visit to your auntie's.

You've got to cut off your head
and stick it on the ground –

then you can step
inside.

$\mathcal{M}$asters say
  we have it easy nowadays:

  Live comfortably at home,
  eat and sleep when you want –

  then sit down
  and close your eyes
  for a couple of hours every day.

In the good old days they used to make a seeker sit on a stool. Every time he moved, the master would whack him with a bamboo stick.

The next day they would tire him out with hard work, then make him sit on a stool – and every time he moved, the master would whack him with a bamboo stick.

The next day they would feed him a big meal, then make him sit on a stool. Every time he moved,

Some people get there
straightaway – others
take decades

to sit still
regardless of pain, tiredness,
overeating, overworking…

the master would whack him
with a bamboo stick.

Then they would make him stay
awake all night – and every time
he moved, the master would whack
him with a bamboo stick.

After that, they would tire him
out with hard work, feed him a
big meal, make him stay awake all
night – and only when he could
keep still would the seeker
be initiated!

*U*nexpected connection –
death and being a true lover.

Fear of withdrawing at will
from the body in meditation?

Kabir reminds us: You want to reach
the home of love!

HINDI SAYING, PRÉM SECTION
jab lagi marné se ᴅarai, tab lagi prémi naahi~;
baʀi door hai prém ghar, samujhi léhu man maahi~.[20]

31

*Y*ou're afraid of death
and you want to be a lover?
Impossible!

It's far away,
the home of love.

But you realize it
inside your mind.

The mystics
see no one as bad

because all they see is God –
in everyone and everything.

And they themselves?
Humility, nothingness

in the face of
God.

HINDI SAYING, DEENTA SECTION
bura jo dékhan mai~ chala, bura na miliya koé;
jo dil khojau~ aapana, mujhsa bura na hoé.

94

32

When I set out looking
for somebody who was bad
I found no one.

Then I searched my own heart:
Oh.

No one, bad like me.

$\mathcal{W}$e are spiritually thirsty

but drinking the water of life
takes humility.

Our growing thirst
may at some point make us
bend…

Or not, as Kabir says!

HINDI SAYING, DEENTA SECTION
*oo~ché paani na ᴛikai, neeché hee ᴛhaihairaaé;
neecha hoé so bhari pivai, oo~cha pyaasaa jaaé.*

33

*W*ater doesn't stay
in high places –
it settles down low.

Are you willing to bend?
Then drink your fill.

Or
stand tall
and go thirsty!

$\mathcal{L}$overs of God are rare.

But when a real lover
finds the Beloved inside,
they merge into the sound and light –

every thought
saturated
in that sweetness:

forever.

HINDI SAYING, GURU SHISHYA KHOJ SECTION
prémi ᴅ*hoo~*ᴅ*hat mai~ phirau~, prémi milai na koé;*
prémi sé prémi milai, vish sé amrit hoé.[21]

34

I set out looking for a lover –
a real lover.
Didn't find even one.

When a lover meets
merges
with a lover

poison
becomes
nectar!

*M*ale elephants are trapped in a pit
by enticing them
with a dummy female elephant
made of straw.

The mind traps us
with illusions of pleasure.

Like the elephant
and like the widow,
we regret

when it's too late!

HINDI SAYING: KG OR GUJARATI[22]

35

*M*ind is an elephant in rut:
it doesn't listen –
until it stumbles into the pit.

A widow
only repents
when she conceives.

The mystics tell stories
and invent sayings
to inspire us

to question
our heavy involvement in the world

and to go into action
towards the spiritual goal
of our life.

*In the 1400s the mystic Nanak
and his companion Mardana
travelled all over India and
beyond, on foot.*

*As they approach one particular
village, they notice a graveyard
that strikes them as curious:
everybody buried there has died
young – at two, three, five, or
twelve at the most.*

*Mardana asks a group of villagers
the reason.*

And those efforts of ours
reflect our level of
spiritual

maturity...

The villagers explain:

We mark the gravestones
with the amount of time each
person spends in remembrance
of the Lord.

Nothing else counts.

*E*motions come and go.

Real love and devotion,
says Kabir

are constant.

HINDI SAYING, PRÉM SECTION
aaya prém kahaa~ gaya, dékha tha sab koé;
chhin rovai chhin me~ ha~sai, so to prém na hoé.

36

I swear love came –
now where's it gone?
Everybody saw it.

Crying one minute,
laughing the next –

you think that's love?

$\mathcal{A}$ssociation
with the master
awakens love and longing.

With love comes patience
for meditation.

With longing comes inner detachment
from the world.

With the satguru comes naam –
the one thing that will dissolve

the mind's desires.

HINDI SAYING, PRÉM SECTION
prém bina dheeraj nahee~, biraih bina bairaag;
satguru bin jaavai nahee~, man mansa ka daag.[23]

37

*W*ithout love – no patience.
Without longing – no detachment.

Without a true teacher
it will not go –

the stain on the mind
of desire.

Shock! The true disciple
is a servant and a pet dog?

Obedience, loyalty, devotion...

Kabir clinches it:
The disciple is leashed
to the master

by love.

HINDI SAYING, SÉVAK AUR DAAS SECTION
sévak kutta guru ka, motiya va ka naa~o;
Dori laagi prém ki, jit khai~chai tit jaao.[24]

38

The servant is a dog
of the master's. He answers
to any name.

He wears the leash
of love. Wherever he's pulled
he goes.

Drily, Kabir describes
the deeply respectful
obedience

and absolute reliance
of a disciple who knows

who the master is.

HINDI SAYING, SÉVAK AUR DAAS SECTION
dur dur karai~ to baahiré, too too karai~ to jaaé;
jyo~ guru raakhai~ tyo~ raihai, jo dévai~ so khaaé.

39

"*G*o away!" –
outside he goes.
"Here, you" –
back he comes.

Whatever
the master gives him –
that's what he eats.

However the master
keeps him –
that's how it is.

*T*ough love.

The master gives the disciple –
inside, outside –
whatever is needed, however painful...

and the strength and support
to handle whatever they have
to go through.

HINDI SAYING, GURUDÉV SECTION
*guru kumhaar sish kumbh hai, gaʀh gaʀh kaaᴅhai khoᴛ;
antar haath sahaar dai, baahar baahai choᴛ.*

40

The master is a potter,
the disciple a pot.

He kneads and kneads,
then throws the clay –

one hand inside, supporting,
the other outside, whacking!

*L*ike Nand Lal
we may get so engrossed in the world
we are carried away by our success.

The company and guidance
of a true mystic protect us
from ourselves –

if we are open.

*Bhai Nand Lal Goya was a
famous poet in Delhi at the court
of the emperor Aurangzeb
in the 1600s.*

*Aurangzeb thinks it would be
an excellent idea to convert
this brilliant poet to Islam.*

*Nand Lal in desperation runs
to Punjab, to Guru Gobind Singh
in Chandigarh. He tells the gate-
keeper to announce him –
with all his impressive titles.*

Full of our own self-importance,
what can we receive?

The master challenges us,
making us aware of our lack of
patience and humility.

He places Nand Lal
in the community kitchen
where everybody

rich and poor
together

works, serves
and eats
side by side...

A message comes back that
Guru Sahib says he is to go to the
free kitchen, the langar.

This goes on for three days.

Finally Nand Lal thinks: I have
come here for shelter as a beggar.
A beggar goes in humility. He
doesn't promote or praise himself.

So he goes to the gate and says,
"Please tell Guru Sahib there is a
beggar at the door who seeks
some alms."

And the Guru calls him.

A true disciple?

Nothing belongs to me –
body, mind, soul, belong to the guru.

And the guru?

A master does not accept
even a penny
for his personal needs.

HINDI SAYING, GURU SHISHYA KHOJ SECTION
sish to aisa chaahiyé, guru sé sab kuchh déi;
guru to aisa chaahiyé, sish sé kachhu na léi.

41

A disciple?
Gives everything
to the master.

A master?
Takes nothing
from the disciple.

*T*here is one in human form
who can give

what is beyond the realm

of reward and punishment.

HINDI SAYING, PRÉM SECTION
hari sé too jani hét kar, kar harijan sé hét;
maal muluk hari dét hai, harijan harihee~ dét.[25]

42

Don't love God,
love his lovers!

The Lord gives you
wealth and property.

His lovers?
They give you God.

*W*e cannot truly love
if we don't have awe –

fear of offending the Beloved.
Doing what the master teaches

is the sweetness
in the practice.

HINDI SAYING, CHITAAVANI SECTION
bhaé bin bhaa'u na upajai, bhaé bin hoé na preeti;
jab hirdé sé bhaé gaya, miτi sakal ras reeti.

43

*I*f you don't feel awe
love doesn't emerge –
and it doesn't deepen, either.

When your heart is empty of fear,
it destroys the sweetness
of your practice.

The mystic doesn't ask
even for liberation or salvation –
the end-goal of most religions.

Kabir highlights the one thing
of value: love and devotion
for the Beloved.

With that,
the devotee has everything.
Without it, nothing.

HINDI SAYING, SÉVAK AUR DAAS SECTION
bhukti mukti maangau~ nahee~, bhakti daan dai mohi~;
aur kachhoo yaachau~ nahee~, nisu din yaachau~ tohi~.

44

I'm not asking
for this liberation thing,
but for the gift
of devotion.

I'm not begging
for anything else –
just you... Day and night:
You.

$\mathcal{F}$rom the spiritual point of view
we are all thirsty.

The oyster is the person
who has reached a level of longing

where they want only
the Beloved –
that rare drop of blue moon rain.

Nothing else
will quench their thirst.

HINDI SAYING, PATIBRATA SECTION
kabeer seep samund ki, raтai piyaas piyaas;
aur boond ko na gaihai, swaanti boond ki aas.[26]

45

*O*yster in the ocean, Kabir –
keeps repeating "Thirsty...
thirsty..."

Its hopes
are in that single drop
of blue moon rain.

It won't accept any other.

*P*sychic powers
are the goal of many yogic paths.

For the devotee,
seeing the master –
inside, outside –

is the be-all
and end-all
on this path of love.

HINDI SAYING, SATSANG SECTION
riddhi siddhi maangau~ nahee~, maangau~ tum pai
yéh; nisu din darsan saadh ka, kaih kabeer mohi~ dé.

46

I'm not asking
for *riddhi-siddhi* psychic powers,
I'm asking you for this:

the darshan of a saint
day and night.

Says Kabir: Please –
give me that.

$\mathcal{L}$ittle interest in the world

and restless,
agonized

without seeing
the Beloved.

HINDI SAYING, BIREH SECTION
nain hamaaré baavaré, chhin chhin loʀai~ tujjh;
na tum milo na mai~ sukhi, aisi bédan mujjh.

47

*M*y eyes have gone mad,
desperate for you.

They don't find you
nor do I find happiness.

That
is the crux of my torment.

What a contrast:
life out in the world
(eat, drink and be merry)

and the life of the devotee:
no sleep,
meditating all night –

yearning for the Beloved.

HINDI SAYING, BIREH SECTION
sukhiyaa sab sa~saar hai, khaavai au sovai;
dukhiyaa daas kabeer hai, jaagai au rovai.

48

*T*he whole world is happy,
eating and sleeping.

This slave Kabir is miserable –
wide awake, weeping.

Going inside, reaching
the radiant form of the master,
spending time in his physical company –

not in the disciple's hands.

The option?
Meditation –
calling again and again

waiting for the master
to open the door.

HINDI SAYING, BIREH SECTION
aay sako~ nahi~ tohi~ pai, sako~ na tujjh bulaaé;
jiyara yo~ laé hoéga, biraih tapaaé tapaaé.

49

I cannot come to you –
if I could
I wouldn't call out to you.

It will take away my life,
all this burning and agonizing
in separation.

Bireh is mysterious.

Kabir has even called it

the most ancient
path to God.

HINDI SAYING, BIREH SECTION
birahaa burahaa mat kaho, birahaa hai sultaan;
ja ghaт biraha na sa~charai, so ghaт jaan masaan.

50

*D*on't say *bireh* is bad –
the pain of separation
is the emperor himself!

A body where the pain
of separation isn't
stirring –

cremation ground.

Every now and then
a devotee may reveal
the intensity

of what is known as *bireh*...

*Ameer Khusrau loved his master
from childhood on.*

*Over time he becomes wealthy
as an outstanding poet, musician,
writer, historian, diplomat —
but throughout he remains
an exceptionally devoted disciple.*

*When his master, Nizamuddin
Auliya, knows his own time has
come, he sends Ameer Khusrau
out of Delhi on some pretext.*

Years before
Nizamuddin had said:

"Don't let Ameer Khusrau
anywhere near my tomb –
he will tear it apart to reach me!"

The disciples buried Ameer Khusrau
in the same tomb as his master.

Ameer Khusrau returns
to hear that his master is dead.
Immediately he goes blind.

He is led to Nizamuddin's tomb,
bows down his head – and dies.

Supreme path,
the path of longing –

burning up
with love

and hope
of union.

HINDI SAYING, BIREH SECTION
birahin oobhee panth sir, panthini poochhai dhaaé;
ék sabad kaho peeu ka, kab ré milaingé aaé.[27]

51

*A*nguished lover
standing on that path of paths,
fainting with the heat.

Another comes running –
What can I do?

Just give me one word
from my Beloved: When

is he coming
to meet me?

*T*here is only one physician

who knows how to heal
the affliction

of a longing heart!

HINDI SAYING, BIREH SECTION
kabeera baid bulaa'iya, pakari ké dékhee baa~hi;
baid na bédan jaana'i, karak karéjé maahi~.

52

*K*abir, they call a doctor...
he takes hold of your wrist,
feels the pulse.

Doctors know nothing
of this disease!

The problem
is inside
the heart.

When love becomes

unceasing –

no words.

HINDI SAYING, PRÉM SECTION
prém prém sab koee kaihai, prém na cheenhai ko'i;
aaʈh paihair bheena raihai, prém kahaavai so'i.

53

*E*verybody talks about love –
love this, love that –
but none of them
has experienced it.

When you've been soaked
with love, not dry for a second
in twenty-four hours –

yes, call that
love.

*M*editation practice
may be long and hard

but ultimately –

pure ecstasy!

HINDI SAYING, PRÉM SECTION
kabeer pyaala prém ka, antar liya lagaaé;
rom rom mé~ rami rahaa, aur amal kya khaaé.

54

Kabir, this cup of love –
when it takes effect inside,
every hair stands on end
with ecstasy.

Permeated with it –
who needs intoxicants!

Mahmood of Ghazni, Afghanistan,
and Ayaaz, the Georgian slave
he made into the king of Lahore,
lived five hundred years before Kabir.

Mystics have told stories
of their love relationship
for centuries

to illustrate
the intensity and depth of love

between a real disciple
and the true master.

EN[28]

The ministers of king Mahmood were jealous of his love for Ayaaz, his favourite slave.

One day the king decides to show them what it is about Ayaaz that makes him his beloved.

The king gives all of them a day off to go out into the city and beyond to enjoy a huge fair that is taking place.

He says: "Be back by six this evening – and bring me a gift."

Most of us lose ourselves
in the fairgrounds of the world,
forgetting the purpose of our life.

The end comes
and we haven't done the one thing
we were asked to –

remember the Beloved

with the gift of attention.

The ministers jump at the chance
of a day without any duties.

Soon they are lost in the fair-
grounds, enjoying themselves
no end.

Suddenly the sun begins to set —
six o'clock is upon them.

A few ministers run as fast as
they can for the palace. Others stop
on the way and quickly buy for
the king the first thing they see.

All of them are late.

Like Ayaaz,
we have the chance in this life

to keep our attention
on the Beloved:

no going and returning –
unwavering.

Love.

And when they enter
the king's chamber, they find
the king with Ayaaz.

Ayaaz is sitting at the feet
of the king.

He never left.

He spent the day with his Beloved –
gazing into his eyes.

$\mathcal{T}$he ecstasy and wonder
of the inner experience
is not to be shared.

If you show it,
you lose it –

priceless wealth.

HINDI SAYING, APAARIKH SECTION
naam ratan dhan paa'i kai, gaa~ʈhi baandh naa khol;
naahi~ paʈan nahi~ paarakhee, nahi~ gaahak nahi~
mol.

55

The jewel of naam –
when you get that wealth
tie it up tight, don't show it
to anyone.

Forget about jewellers
and assayers
and buyers
and appraisers.

It has no price.

*I*nner merging
    goes against everything
    we see and hear all around us.

You say No to the world.

Kabir says you can do it –

with faith
    in the presence
    of the master. Inside.

HINDI SAYING, NAAM SECTION
surati samaavai naam mé~, jag sé raihai udaas;
kaiha kabeer guru charan mé~, driʀh raakhau bisvaas.[29]

56

To merge surat in the name
pull back from the world.

Says Kabir, you'll need
to keep your faith

firm in the lotus feet
of the master.

The mystics willingly
share the teachings with seekers –

but naam is never sold,
nor can it be bought at any price.

The master wanders the world,
radiant with the energy
of the word –

needing no introduction
to contact the people
he is to give the treasure to.

HINDI SAYING, APAARIKH SECTION
*jaha~ gaahak taha~ mai~ nahee~, mai~ taha~ gaahak
naahee~; parichay bin phoolaa~ phirai, pakar sabad ki
baahi~.*[30]

57

*W*here there's a buyer
I disappear. I exist only
where customers are not.

Without introduction
I wander around
bursting at the seams

because I caught hold
of shabd!

The lover is the rare person
who gives all

regardless of what
or whether they receive anything
in return.

Love is not
a commercial transaction.
It's giving –

opening the heart,
serene

letting go.

HINDI SAYING, PRÉM SECTION[31]

58

You're thirsty for love?
Cut off your head!

If you do this, there's a chance
of getting something.

Maybe!

What should we be like?

How should we behave?

Kabir explores the possibilities

and discards one analogy
after another.

HINDI SAYINGS, DEENTA SECTION
kabeera roRa ho'i rahu baaT ka, taji man ka abhimaanu;
aisa koee daasu ho'i, tahi milé bhagvaanu (1).

kabeer roRa hua ta kia bha'ia, panthi ka'u dukhu déi;
aisa téra daasu hai, jiu dharni mahi khéhi (2).

*Kabir was once asked what
an ideal disciple would be like.
He said:*

*They would be like stones on a
roadway, trampled all day: no ego.
That's the kind of devotee who
would meet the Lord.*

*Then again, stones hurt
the travellers' feet…*

*So your devotee would be like
dust on the ground.*

And he goes on
discarding the options,
always finding something wrong.

Finally he gives up.
There is no image
for how the disciple needs to be.

Instead, says Kabir:
You need to become
like God.

HINDI SAYINGS, DEENTA SECTION
kabeer khéh huee ta'u kia bha'ia, ja'u URI *laagai ang;*
hari janu aisa chaahié, jiu paani sarabang (3).

kabeer paani hua ta kia bha'ia, seera taata ho'i;
hari janu aisa chaahié, jaisa hari hee ho'i (4).[32]

*Then again, dust flies up and
sticks to every part of you…*

*Hm… A true lover of the Lord?
They would need to be like water:
moulding itself to all things.*

*Then again, water can be hot
and water can be cold…*

*What can I tell you?
The lover of God needs to become
just like God!*

*T*he beauty of having
a living master, a true teacher
of the time

is that you can
see him, talk to him,
be inspired by him…

Miss him…

Love him!

59

*I*f the master
were to meet me this time,
I'd tell him all my pains –
with tears.

I'd lay my head on his feet
and say…
what longs
to be said.

*H*opes,
 dreams,
 imagining,
 memories –

 the joy
 that one day
 it will happen.

HINDI SAYING, BIREH SECTION
*so din kaisa hoéga, guru gaihengé baa~hi; apanaa kari
baiThaavahee~, charan ka~val ki chhaa~hi.*[33]

60

*H*ow will that day be –
when the master
takes hold of my arms...

makes me totally his own...

gives me shelter
at his lotus feet.

*L*ove on the bhakti path –
remembrance,
dying or living:

silent action

awareness

presence of the Beloved

HINDI SAYING, BIREH SECTION
too mati jaanai beesaroo~, preeti ghaтai mam chitt;
maroo~ to tum sumirat maroo~, jioo~ to sumiroo~ nitt.

61

I don't know how
to forget you
or how to lessen
the feelings in my heart.

If I die, I'll go with simran –
remembering
you.

If I live – I'll go on with
simran: always
you.

$\mathcal{L}$ove is not easy.
Nor is it automatic.
There is work to be done.

Love pulls the disciple
to meditate. And to keep going
regardless.

And meditation flowers
into that painful joy –

bireh.

HINDI SAYING, BIREH SECTION
nainan to jhari laa'iya, raiha⊤ bahai nisu baas;
papeeha jyo~ piu piu ra⊤ai, piya milan ki aas.[34]

62

*T*ears streaming
from my eyes –
persian wheel
pouring day and night.

Cuckoo calling
"My love, my love".
Just one hope:
to meet the Beloved.

*L*onging
is intense:

The Beloved becomes
one's natural element...

Death,
without him.

HINDI SAYING, BIREH SECTION
birahini déi sandésara, suno hamaaré peeo;
jal bin machchhi kyo~ jiyé, paani mé~ ka jeeo.[35]

63

*M*essage
 from anguished lover:

Listen, my Beloved –
how do you expect a fish
to stay alive out of water?

And how do you expect me
to stay alive
under water?

$\mathcal{T}$he eternal way
to God-realization:
love and longing.

And the response
to that incurable pain –

suddenly the Beloved,
inside.

Fulfilled!

HINDI SAYING, SÉVAK AUR DAAS SECTION
daas dukhi to hari dukhi, aadi ant tihu~ kaal;
palak ék mé~ pragaт hvai, chhin mé~ karai nihaal.

64

When the slave is unhappy,
God is unhappy.
It's always been that way –
always will be.

In a moment he appears.
In seconds lifts you up –
and gives you great
joy.

*F*orget the ocean:
the oyster wants that one
unique drop of rain.

Forget even the outcome –
the pearl
of spiritual liberation.

The lover?

Happy
with Beloved.

HINDI SAYING, PRÉM SECTION
saadh seep samudra ké, satguru swaanti bund;
trisha ga'i ik bund sé, kya lé karau~ samund.[36]

65

$\mathcal{D}$isciple – an oyster
in the ocean. Master:
the drop of blue moon rain.

My thirst was quenched
with a single drop.
What do I need
with an ocean?

*F*ifty years before Kabir,
the mystic Naamdev became known
for his childlike faith in God.

The mystics say
the saints see God in everyone
and everything.

All calamities,
even losing one's precious lunch,
are seen as the Lord.

Literally!

One day, the mystic Naamdev
sits down in the shade of a tree
and unwraps his simple lunch
of two chapatis and a small pot
with a few drops of ghee.

A stray dog runs past
and grabs the chapatis.

Naamdev jumps up and chases
after the dog, calling out:

"Wait, dear Lord! Don't eat
them dry – take the ghee, too!"

The simple wish
of the lover

for the Beloved to come,
full of love, and for
the two of them

to spend
timeless time together,
silently sharing –

deeply content.

HINDI SAYING, BINTI SECTION
méré satguru milaingé, poochhaingé kusalaat;
aadi ant ki sab kahau~, ur antar ki baat.

66

*W*hen I meet my beloved master
he will ask me how I am.

I will tell him everything
from beginning to end:

all those
matters of the heart.

*A*s a contemporary mystic puts it:

All the hard work
of struggling with the mind

of initial dryness in simran
and lack of apparent results
in meditation –

"It's worth it…"

for that inner tryst
where only lover
and Beloved
exist.

HINDI SAYING, PRÉM SECTION
neeché loin kari raha'u, lé saajan ghaт maahi~;
sabh ras khéla'u pia sa'u, kisi lakhaava'u naahi~.

67

I'll take the friend inside,
then close my eyes
and keep them shut

so no one else can see him.

What bliss –
my Beloved and I,
we play.

When the master comes by,
inside or outside

there is an outpouring
of grace.

Love takes over –
even the plants go crazy!

HINDI SAYING, GURUDÉV SECTION
kabeer baadal prém ko, ham par barasyo aaé;
antar bhee~jee aatma, haro bhayo banaraaé.

68

$\mathcal{K}$abir,
the cloud of love came by.
The rain poured down on me.

Soul got soaked
inside

and every plant in sight
has turned a brilliant green!

The lover is lost
in the Beloved…

sees nothing else,
knows nothing else,
thinks nothing else –

lit up inside
with that tenderness
and glory.

HINDI SAYING, PARICHAY SECTION
laalee méré laal ki, jit dékhau~ tit laal;
laalee dékhan mai~ ga'i, mai~ bhee ho ga'i laal.[37]

69

$\mathcal{T}$he radiance of my jewel,
my darling, my shining one –
wherever I look, that's all I see:

Radiance…
Beloved…

When I set out to take a look
at that radiance of his,
I too became radiant!

*I*dentity lost,
  there is now
  only the Beloved –

  no room for anything else.

HINDI SAYING, PRÉM SECTION
*jab mai~ tha tab guru nahee~, ab guru hai~ ham
naahi~; prém gali ati saa~kari, ta me~ do na samaahi~.*

70

When I was,
the master was not.

Now the master is,
I am not.

The lane of love is so narrow
there's not room for two.

This story of the Buddhist teacher
and the villagers is about
listening.

In fact, the whole
of the inner way

is about listening.

*There was once a famous
Buddhist teacher. A nearby
village invites him to come
and give a talk.*

*On the appointed day the villagers
gather in great excitement.*

*The teacher arrives, sits down
and asks them: "Do you know
what I have come here to say?"*

*The villagers look at one another
and think they had better sound
prepared, so they say: Yes.*

All of us tend to be know-it-alls:

we have seen it on the internet,
heard it on the radio or TV,
even read a book on it!

Where is there room to learn
when we come to the masters
like that?

How can we hear
what the mystics say –

much less act
on what they tell us!

The teacher says, "If you know
what I have come to say,
there's no need for me to stay."

And he leaves.

A delegation goes to him and
invites him to come another
day, so he does.

This time he again asks them,
"Do you know what I have
come here to say?"

The villagers are prepared for this,
so they say: No.

Cleverness, too,
must go.

Bit by bit
the masters maneuver us

emptying our mind...

The teacher says, "If you don't
know what I have come to say,
there's no need for me to stay."

And he leaves.

Another delegation goes to him
and invites him to come
on another day, so he does.

This time he again asks them:
"Do you know what I have come
here to say?"

Well prepared this time, half
the villagers say Yes, the other half
say No.

…until we are ready at last
even for a moment

to hear and receive.

As the mystics say:

The masters are humble givers.
We are proud beggars.

But the teacher says, "In that case,
the ones who know can tell the ones
who don't know." And he gets up
and leaves.

In great confusion a delegation
of villagers goes to the teacher.
They beg him to come and
talk to them one more time.

He comes. He asks the question.
The villagers look at him
and say nothing.

He begins to speak.

*L*osing one's identity
comes from
love for the Beloved.

Receptive.

You... Only you...

Immersed like that,
where would the mind
want to go!

HINDI SAYING, LAV SECTION
too~ too~ karta too~ bhaya, tujh mé~ raha samaaé;
tujh maahee~ man mili raha, ab kahu~ anat na jaaé.

71

You... You...
I've repeated you so much
I've become you now,
completely merged
in you.

My mind –
immersed
in you
again and again:
where else can it go!

*H*ow strange and wonderful
to have no "I"!

Kabir describes
the devotee as puzzled –

only the Beloved
is.

HINDI SAYING, PRÉM SECTION
sunu sakhee peea mahi~ jeeu basai, jeea basai ki peeu;
*jeeu peeu boojha'u nahee~, gha*T *mahi~ jeeu ki peeu.*

72

*L*isten, dear friend:
Does my soul live in the Beloved
or does he live in my soul?

I can't tell the difference
between soul and Beloved –

is it my soul
or my Beloved
in me?

*A*t the final stage
no separation
or surrender:

only the Beloved.

All the years of effort –
trying, failing, letting go –

all his, all him.

HINDI SAYING, BINTI SECTION
méra mujh mé~ kachhu nahee~, jo kachhu hai so tujjh;
téra tujh ko sau~paté, ka laagat hai mujjh.

73

There's nothing of mine
in me.

Whatever there is
is yours.

In returning yours to you
what credit to me!

$\mathcal{H}$ow to attain
  Kabir's carefree state?

He gives a hint:

Let God do your worrying!

HINDI SAYING, VISHVAAS SECTION
*kabeer kya mai~ chintahoo~, mam chinté kya hoé;
méri chinta hari karai, chinta mohi~ na koé.*[38]

74

$\mathcal{K}$abir, why should I worry?
What would worrying do?

It's God
who does my worrying.

It leaves me
carefree.

$\mathcal{A}$ young woman once asked a master
whether simran is enough
if you are attacked

or whether you should train
in martial arts
for self-defence.

The master smiled and said:
It's not a question of simran,
it's the lack of it!

If you have faith
in your master…

And in true Kabir style
he answered with this parable
of the village priest
and the simple woman…

There was once a village priest
who gave an inspiring discourse
on faith.

He tells everybody:
"With faith you can achieve
anything in the world."

There is a simple woman
who hears what he says. She lives
on the far side of the river,
so she needs to cross the river
whenever she wants to visit
the temple.

The simplicity
of faith –

no questioning,
analysing,
weighing pros and cons!

Instead –

serene confidence,
surrender,
action.

Remembering what the priest said,
she prays and then walks across the
water.

At the temple she bows at the feet
of the priest and thanks him
for teaching her everything.
Then she invites him to a meal
to express her gratitude.

The priest is only too happy
to accept. "But how do you get
across the river?"

"You taught me that with faith
anything is possible," she says —
and walks across.

The master ended the story
by saying to the young woman:

If we have that faith in the Lord
he will take care of us... *if*
you have that faith.

And with a smile he added:

But you can still try your karate!

The priest thinks,
If she can do it, why not me?
After all, I am a priest!

He takes two or three steps
and thinks, She is mad –
and down he goes!

When the radiant form
becomes visible

inside, disciples may see him
outside, everywhere.

Seeing the Beloved
becomes

their lifeline.

HINDI SAYING, PRÉM SECTION
aaтh jaam chausaтhi ghari, tua nirakhat raihai jeeu;
neeché loin kiu kara'u, sabh ghaт dékha'u piu.

75

*T*wenty-four hours,
every second,
I stay alive by gazing at you.

Why should I close my eyes?
In everybody
it's the Beloved I see!

$\mathcal{K}$abir reminds us:
Why think of separation
and messages to one who is far away —

the Beloved couldn't be closer!
He is inside you,
he knows everything about you.

Find him!

HINDI SAYING, PRÉM SECTION
preetam ko patiyaa~ likhoo~, jo kahu~ hoé bidés;
tan mé~ man mé~ nain mé~, taa ko kahaa sandés.

220

76

I would write my Beloved
a letter – if he had gone
to another country.

Right inside
my body,
my mind,
my eyes –

A message?
What for!

What most disciples see
of the master, the physical form,
is not real.

Unshakeable faith comes
from experiencing what is real –
the shabd master.

Those lucky ones don't talk about it
or try to convince others,
because they know

everybody needs to experience
truth
for themselves.

HINDI: KABIR SAMAGRA, P.772; ALSO ADI GRANTH
jo deesai so to naahee~, hai so kahaa na jaaé;
bin dékhai parteet na aavai, kaihai na ko patiyaana.

77

*W*hat you see doesn't exist.
What is
can't be put into words.

Without seeing there's no faith.
And those who have seen
are silent:

confident beyond words.

When love and longing
evolve

the Beloved cannot resist –
he longs for his lovers

as much as they
long for him.

HINDI SAYING, NIDRA SECTION
piu piu kaihi kaihi kookiyé, na so'iyé israar;
raat divas ké kookaté, kabahunk lagai pukaar.

78

*B*eloved... *B*eloved...

Go on calling
again and again.
Don't go to sleep, persist!

If you call day and night,
he just might start calling
you.

*F*rom the beginning
meditation is about
giving pleasure to the Beloved.

First, simply by showing up –

spreading simran before him
like petals on a wedding bed.

And then –
it evolves…

in secret,
inside.

HINDI SAYING, PRÉM SECTION
naino~ ki kari koᴛhari, putali palang bichhaaé;
palako~ ki chik ᴅaari kai, piya ko liya rijhaaé.

79

*T*urn your eyes into a secret room.
Inside the pupil spread a bed
with flowers.

Now gently close the curtain
of your eyelashes

and do everything you know
to bring pleasure
to the Beloved!

*A*bsorbing naam –

drinking in
the sound, the essence:

Kabir says
you never come back down…

Body and mind function here
but consciousness –
far beyond.

HINDI SAYING, PRÉM SECTION
piya ras piya so jaaniyé, utarai nahee~ khumaar;
naam amal maata raihai, piyai ami ras saar.[39]

80

Drink it down, this juice,
if you really want to know
your Beloved.

The effect? Never wears off!
You'll stay high,
intoxicated on naam

once you've drunk
the nectar juice –
the essence.

*U*nimaginable bliss
in that oneness –

merged
completely
in beauty and joy:

the radiant form.

HINDI SHABDAVALI, VIREH AUR PRÉM
*piya ko roop kahaa~ lag barano~, roopahi maahi~
samaanee; jo rang rangé sakal chhabi chhaké, tan man
sabhee bhulaanee.*[40]

81

*H*ow can I describe
the beauty of my Beloved
when I've totally merged
in that beauty, his form!

Whatever colour it is, this love,
he's dyed me in it.
And his radiance?
Drank it up – drunk!

Body, mind, all of it:
forgotten.

The ordinary person
is satisfied with everyday basics –
the bread of the world.

And then there are
others –

who want more
than anything the world
can offer.

A gaggle of beggars sits
at the gateway to the king's palace,
calling out for alms.

The king sends his minister
to find out what they want.

The minister comes back
with their request: "Bread, sire."

"Give them bread and send them
away. But there's one who sounds
different — ask him what he
wants."

They long only to see
the Beloved –
their king.

And the Beloved?

He loves such lovers.
He loves their presence –

the focus,
their love.

So he keeps them waiting
at his door.

He wants the intensity
of their longing, day and night

so he can give them
himself.

The minister arranges for the beggars to be fed and sent on their way – except for the one who is different.

The minister asks: "What is it you want?"

And returns with the answer: "If you please, sire, the beggar says – I want to see the face of my king."

"Good. Let him wait. I like the sound of his voice."

$\mathcal{T}$he world is an orgy –

we are surrounded by temptations.
Everything pulls our attention out.

Sacrifice all of it, says Kabir,
to stay in the presence

of the master.

HINDI SAYING, SATSANG SECTION
kabeer sangat saadh ki, jau ki bhoosi khaaé;
kheer khaa~ᴅ bhojan milai, saakat sang na jaaé.[41]

82

*K*abir, stay
in the company of a saint
even if you get
rubbish to eat.

Delicious foods
and your favourite desserts –
don't go near them
in an orgy.

*K*abir urges us
to give time
to meditation while we can.

And to give
more time –

now!

HINDI SAYING, CHITAAVANI SECTION
looτi sakai to looτi lé, raam naam ki looτ;
phiri paachhai pachhatahugé, praan jaahingé chhooτ.

83

*R*ansack, raid, rob
while you can –
all the treasure
of God's name!

Otherwise you'll regret it
in the end
when your life breath
drops you.

When we are absorbed
in naam, in love with the sound,
we automatically overcome

the mind's five perversions –
lust, anger, greed,
attachment, ego.

There's nothing left:
body-mind and senses
consumed in the fire

of passion for the divine.

HINDI SAYING, GURU SHISHYA KHOJ SECTION
aisa ko'i na mila, ghar dé aapan jaraaé;
paa~cho larika paтaki ké, raihai naam lau laaé.[42]

84

I've never met anybody
who has burnt down
their own house.

What happens?
You finally crush that gang,
the Five Boys.

You're totally absorbed,
enflamed
by the name.

☙

*H*ow many people
are willing to let the master
rescue them?

Most of us think
we are doing just fine!

HINDI SAYING, GURU SHISHYA KHOJ SECTION
ham dékhat jag jaat hai, jag dékhat ham jaahi~;
aisa ko'i na mila, pakari chhuʀaavai baahi~.[43]

85

To me,
it looks like the world
is drowning. To them,
it looks like I am!

I've yet to meet anybody
who will grab my arm
and pull me out –

nor let me help them
either.

The mind is a lover
of pleasure.

The mystics say:
All it takes is one taste

one glimpse

and the mind becomes
your friend.

HINDI SAYING, KARNI AUR KATHNI SECTION
kathanee meeᴛhee khaa~ᴅ see, karnee bish ki loé;
kathanee taji karnee karai, to bish sé amrit hoé.

86

*P*eople love to talk
about the path.
It tastes so sweet,
and the practice – bitter
as poison.

Quit talking, my friend,
and do the practice –
poison will turn
into nectar!

*T*he masters
have burnt ego and separateness –
their identity is the divine!

Radiating that energy,
they ignite with divine passion
anybody who wishes to go with them.

HINDI SAYING, GURU SHISHYA KHOJ SECTION
ham ghar jaara aapana, looka leenha haath;
ab ghar jaarau~ tahi~ ka, jo chalai hamaaré saath.[44]

87

My house –
I've burnt it down.

These flames?
It's the torch in my hand.

I'm off to set fire
to the house of anybody
who wants to go with me!

$\mathcal{T}$he time

is now!

HINDI SAYING, NIDRA SECTION
kabeer soya kya karai, jaagi ké japo dayaar;
ék dinaa hai sovana, lambé pair pasaar.

88

Kabir, what
are you sleeping for?
Wake up, meditate
on the compassionate one!

A day will come
when you can sleep all you want –
legs stretched out
so comfortably.

The story of the ministers
is attributed to the taoist tradition –

the mystic Lao-tse,
about seventeen hundred years
before Kabir.

As would-be disciples,
we are the two ministers,
servants of the king –

and this life
is our chance
to redeem ourselves.

There were once two ministers
accused of a crime punishable
by death.

The king decides to give them
another chance. He calls for a rope
to be stretched tight between the
tops of two hills – and announces
that if the ministers can walk
the tightrope, they will be forgiven.

One minister spends the night
trembling in fear, not able even
to pray or drink his morning tea.

Faced
with our own certain death,
we can avoid thinking about it

and then
be consumed with fear
when it's too late –

or we can live in such a way
that we meet death
with focus and calm.

The other minister, knowing
he knows nothing about tightrope
walking and that he can do
nothing to change this in the few
hours remaining, decides to go
to sleep. He gets up in the morning,
calm and refreshed.

A great crowd gathers to witness
the extraordinary event. The two
ministers pull straws and the
tranquil man goes first.

He steps onto the tightrope
and calmly walks, and walks, and
walks, looking much as if he were
taking a morning stroll.

The tightrope walk
of life is challenging:

one slip
and we're in trouble.

The master-king is there
all the time, watching.

He has reduced the punishment
for our previous actions –

and is more than willing
to forgive.

Eventually he reaches the far side.
The professional acrobats and
tightrope walkers in the crowd
can't believe it – such a long
distance, such a great height,
and the man has never walked
a tightrope before!

The minister bows low to the king.
The king inclines his head in
forgiveness.

Meanwhile the other minister
is shaking with fear. He shouts out
to the first minister:

"How did you do it?"

We just need to walk
the way
of moderation:

neither leaning
to the right,
nor leaning
to the left!

The reply comes:

"I walked as I always do:
balanced – neither leaning to
the right, nor leaning to the left…"

*R*eal mystics never sleep.
When they appear to be sleeping,
even snoring

they are awake, aware
inside.

Kabir says, You too can be
at that level where simran goes on
by itself all the time –

attention
inside.

HINDI SAYING, NIDRA SECTION
jaagat sé sovan bhalaa, jo ko'i jaanai soé;
antar lau laagi rahai, saihaijai sumiran hoé.[45]

89

Sleeping
is better than staying awake –
if you know how
to sleep.

Inside –
your attention fully absorbed,
simran going on
automatically.

$\mathcal{R}$eality check:

We think we meditate,
but the moment we relax
we go right off to sleep –

unless, says Kabir,
we are otherwise occupied!

HINDI SAYING, NIDRA SECTION
kabeer khaalik jaagata, aur na jaagai koé;
kau jaagai vishaya bhaRa, kai daas bandagi soya.

90

*K*abir,
the Creator is awake
but nobody else.

Everybody is either awake
busy indulging

or fast asleep
at devotions.

*T*he battle
is intense
and may take a lifetime –

bringing the attention at will
into the inner practice

and losing awareness
of ego, self, senses.

That takes a warrior, says Kabir.

HINDI SAYING, BHAKTI SECTION
*kaamee krodhee laalachee, in té~ bhakti na hoé;
bhakti karai koee soorama, jaati baran kul khoé.*[46]

91

*I*f you're into lust,
 anger or greed,
 you're not capable of
 devotion.

It takes a warrior
 to do the practice of devotion.

Name, family, race –
 your whole identity:
 gone.

Wherever a devotee takes birth,
however despised by society
they may be –

their devotion:
priceless.

HINDI SAYING, BHAKTI SECTION
bhakti beej binsai nahee~, aa'i paʀai jo chol;
kanchan jo bishʈa paʀai, ghaʈai na taa ko mol.[47]

92

The seed of devotion
is never destroyed,
it doesn't matter which body
it falls into.

Like a nugget of gold
that drops
into shit –
so what?

It doesn't lose its value.

*O*uter worship
is a karmic death warrant –
it involves rebirth into the world.

Liberation? That requires something
quite different.

But most of us, says Kabir,
are simply
not interested.

HINDI SAYING, KARM-KAA~D SECTION
karam phand jag phandiya, jap tap pooja dhyaan;
jéhi sabad té~ mukti havai, so na parai pahichaan.

93

The world is caught
in a noose. They love rituals –
love worshipping, praying,
chanting. Even love penances!

Nobody tries to realize
the word. But that shabd
is what takes you
to freedom.

$\mathcal{H}$undreds of folktales
in the Middle East, Africa
and Afghanistan feature a character
like Mullah Nasruddin.

Some say Nasruddin
is based on a mystic who lived in the 1300s.

Here, Nasruddin
in a bumbling way
shows how fixated we are

on looking everywhere outside
for the truth
when all the time it's inside

hidden in the darkness
at our own door.

EN[48]

*O*ne night Mullah Nasruddin
drops the key to his house
at the door.

*A friend finds him under a
lamppost, searching for something
on the ground. "What are you
looking for, Nasruddin?"*

"The key to my house."

*They both search in vain. "Are you
sure this is where you dropped it?"*

*"No, no, it wasn't here — but it's
way too dark to find at my door."*

$\mathcal{A}$ thousand books

or two lines –

the inner practice
is what counts.

Do that
and you find truth.

HINDI SAYING, UPDÉSH SECTION
*kabeer aadhee saakhi yaha, koтi granth kari jaan;
naam satt jag jhooтh hai, surat sabad paihichaan.*[49]

94

*K*abir, these two lines
   sum up a thousand scriptures:

Naam is true, the world is false.
Recognize it through surat shabd.

The inner sound
is unique:

here in the world

but unlike everything else –
everlasting.

BAAVAN AKHRI, ADI GRANTH, P.340:1
*baavan achhar lok trai, sabhu kachhu in hee maahi~;
éh akhar khiri jaahi~gé, o'i akhar in mahi~ naahi~.*[50]

95

*L*etters of the alphabet –
how far do they reach?
At most, the three worlds:
all that, they contain.

These syllables –
gone in a moment. That
syllable? It's not
among them.

$\mathcal{M}$erge in God now,
while alive.

When we're dead and buried –
too late
to transform.

HINDI SAYING, BIREH SECTION
mooé peechhé mat milau, kaihai kabeera raam;
loha maaτi mili gaya, tab paaras kéhi kaam.[51]

96

Don't wait till I'm dead
to meet me, God!
So says Kabir.

When iron is buried in earth
what use is the touch
of an alchemists' stone?

*M*ystics like Kabir give their lives
  to meeting the needs of seekers...

they travel far to be with them

they charge no money

they are not interested
in name or fame

What *do* they want?

The *mystic Nanak travelled so*
widely, he became well known –
and sometimes his reputation
for sharing unorthodox teachings
preceded him.

One day as he reaches the gateway
of a certain town, he is met by a
delegation holding a cup of water,
full to the brim.

It is a message from the elders
to say there are enough saints and
teachers in their town – no room
for any more.

To help us

on the inner way.

EN[52]

*Nanak picks up a rose petal, places
it on top of the water and sends
the cup back.*

The rose – the Beloved…

There is always room for more.

*O*uter satsang,
  inner satsang —

  inestimable.

HINDI SAYING, SATSANG SECTION
ék ghaʀi aadhi ghaʀi, aadhi hoo sé aadh;
kabeer sangati saadh ki, kaʈai koʈi aparaadh.[53]

97

A couple of hours…
Or half of that.
Or even half of half an hour!

Kabir, those moments
in the company of a saint –

they free you from trillions
of transgressions.

Can we make ourselves
God-realized?

The path, the master,
the effort, discipline, devotion –
it's his love, his grace, his pull.

With humility
and a tinge of humour
Kabir gives all credit to his Lord.

HINDI SAYING
na kachhu kiya na kari saka, na karné jog sareer;
jo kacchu kiya saahib kiya, ta té~ bhaya kabeer.[54]

98

I did nothing –
nor could I:
this body isn't capable
of that!

Whatever has been done,
it's my Lord who did it.
That's how I became
Kabir.

*S*pirituality
may not be fully accessible to us
straightaway.

But as our attention shifts
to what is inside –
soul, Beloved, God –

we lose awareness
of body and mind,
temple and spire.

The senses go thirsty
when you have tasted
shabd.

HINDI SAYING, RAS SECTION
jihi sar ghaʀa na ᴅoobata, ab mai~ gal mali nhaa'i;
déval booʀa kalas soo~, pa~shi tisaaee jaa'i.[55]

99

The lake
where I couldn't dip
a bucket before, I splash
and play – all the dirt
washing away.

The temple sinks
along with its spire.
The birds go
thirsty.

The drop of consciousness
is attached to the one –

the wave, the master.

And from there becomes one
with the One within all:

the ocean.

HINDI SAYING, PARICHAY SECTION
mai~ laaga us ék sé, ék bhaya sab maahi~;
sab méra mai~ saban ka, tahaa~ doosra naahi~.[56]

100

*A*ttached –
I joined the one:
I became the One inside all.

Everything is mine,
I belong to all,
where there is
no other.

$\mathcal{W}$hen we lose
our separate identity, our twoness

in the oneness of the One

there is nothing more to say:
we have done it.

End of story!

HINDI SAYING, PARICHAY SECTION
kaihaina tha so kaihi diya, ab kachhu kaha na jaaé;
ék raha dooja gaya, dariya laihair samaaé.

101

Kabir has said
what he needed to say –
now nothing to add.

One remains,
two has gone –

the wave has merged
in the sea.

EXPLORATIONS

GLOSSARY

alchemists' stone   *paaras:* The philosophers' stone, *lapis philosophorum*, said to turn base metal into gold at a touch; associated with immortality and the elixir of life. For bhakti mystics the true master is the alchemist or philosopher, and his stone is the "touch" of naam on the mind. Kabir points out that this vital contact needs to take place while disciple and master are alive, not after death.

Beloved   The master, the friend, the Lord, the shabd or shabd master.

bhakti   Devotion. Bhakti disciple, bhakti mystic, bhakti tradition: *see* **naam bhakti tradition**

bireh   The intense pain of separation from the Beloved.

blue moon rain   According to Indian mythology, a pearl forms inside an oyster if it receives a drop of rain when the moon is in Swaati or Swaanti (Arcturus). This rare occurrence symbolizes the moment when the disciple meets the master inside: the threshold to complete liberation of the soul – the pearl of great price. The Hindi word for pearl, *moti*, is related to *mukti*, liberation.

clay pot   *ghaт, ghaaт, ghaʀaa:* Large water pot made from unbaked clay (cheap, disposable); the body.

consciousness   In the bhakti understanding, soul is consciousness – a drop of the ocean of consciousness, which is God. At the ordinary level of human experience our consciousness is shrouded; we perceive very little beyond the physical surface. At the stage of full consciousness or realization, soul is free from its coverings (physical and mental) and attains to total consciousness. Indian mystics like Kabir, Nanak, Paltu, Tulsi and Shiv Dayal Singh use a special word for consciousness: *surat*, synonymous with attention, the inner faculty of hearing, the soul.

darshan   Seeing, beholding, gazing: Looking at the master, inside oneself or outside, with attention so absorbed in the master that one is conscious of nothing else.

desire   Our desires and expectations regarding people, places and things of the world have to be fulfilled – according to the karmic law of cause and effect. Desires become the fundamental impulsion, the karmic attraction, that brings the soul back to lifetime after lifetime in the world.

devotion, bhakti   Devotion begins with love of the master and ends with love of naam, the name. According to mystics like Kabir, the particular focus of the devotional practice is inner attuning and oneness in shabd or naam (the word or name) through séva (service) and meditation.

diviner   The master is the expert in locating and revealing to the disciple the hidden treasure, the thing – shabd or naam, within.

elements   The five traditional humours: earth, water, fire, air, ether.

essence   *See* **shabd**

eye centre   Focal point in the forehead for meditation, also referred to as the eye, pupil, heart.

fire   Divine love, inner light.

freedom   *See* **liberation**

friend   The master, the Beloved.

guru   Teacher, master; an enlightener. Traditional derivation: the light-filled presence (*ru*) in the darkness of ignorance (*gu*).

head   Ego. *See also* **mind**

home of love   The supreme level of consciousness, God-realization. The home of the saints or fully realized mystics, it is considered the origins and therefore the real home of every soul.

house   Ego, mind, identity; sometimes symbolizes our sense of separateness from others and from God.

karma   Lit. action: The universal law of cause and effect; reaping what we have sown, both negative and positive. The karmic law works in tandem with the law of transmigration (lifetimes spent in any of numerous life forms). Both laws together keep the soul imprisoned in an unending series of lifetimes in the lower regions – the physical, astral and causal worlds. Desires and actions in previous lives influence our present life; desires and actions in the present influence our future destiny.

liberation   In the bhakti tradition liberation refers to the attainment of spiritual levels of consciousness beyond the sphere of mind with its laws of karma and transmigration.

love   God is love; the goal or destination of the naam bhakti path is to become more and more attuned to the pure spiritual frequency of divine love, the shabd or naam, and merge in it at the highest levels of consciousness.

Soul (initiate) and shabd (master) are often described as lover/beloved, bride/groom, wife/husband; the non-physical union or consummation of their "marriage" (initiation) takes place when the drop of soul merges in the wave of shabd, the master, which leads to their oneness in the ocean of shabd or God-realization – completing the soul's return to its original state of love and oneness in God, the source, the home of love.

master   In the naam bhakti tradition the mystic teacher is a living master who gives seekers the inner connection with shabd or naam and guides them to the highest levels of consciousness – self-realization and God-realization.

meditation   A practice of inner focusing.

merge   The bhakti practice is about merging surat (consciousness, soul) in shabd (word, sound) at higher and higher levels of consciousness, sometimes expressed as merging in shabd after shabd.

mind   Bhakti mystics differentiate body *(tan)*, mind *(man)*, and soul *(rooh* or *aatma)* or consciousness *(surat)*. Mind is inanimate software: a tool, not an entity – powered and enlivened by the energy of soul; unenlightened or lower mind is identified with the body and ego, I-ness, self.

mystic   Generally speaking a mystic is somebody who carries out an inner spiritual practice with the goal of realizing the inner mysteries. Mystics in different traditions adopt a wide range of methods and techniques to achieve their particular goals.

In the naam bhakti tradition, the goal is self-realization and God-realization through the practice of meditating on shabd or naam (word, name). The mystic *(sant,* saint) is a disciple who has achieved it.

While there may be dozens of such fully realized mystics living unobtrusively here and there, the master is the one who has been appointed by his predecessor during his lifetime to carry on the work of initiating seekers and providing inner and outer spiritual guidance.

naam, name, the name of God, the primal name   The divine power that is one with God and that creates and sustains the universe; audible and visible within us as sound and light. It is referred to by mystics with many names, such as spirit, word (shabd, kalma, logos), essence, music, sound, truth, tao, secret, voice.

naam bhakti tradition Various independent lines of mystics in India, traceable from at least the 1100s to present time (including teachers from a variety of religious backgrounds), who practise and teach the way of attuning and then merging individual consciousness in the divine power they call name or word, naam or shabd.

name(s), repeating the name(s) *See* **simran**

nectar Shabd; the sweetness and immortalizing effect of the shabd power; the experience of drinking and merging with shabd at subtle levels of consciousness.

poison The downward tendencies of the mind, including the five passions (lust, anger, greed, attachment, ego); seeking self-gratification through the senses.

primal name *See* **naam**

pupil *See* **eye centre**

radiant form The astral or light form of the teacher.

rebirth *See* **karma**

sacrifice In the naam bhakti tradition there are no outward rituals, ceremonies or sacrificial offerings. Sacrifice is inner: living a disciple's way of life while also fulfilling all one's obligations and responsibilities in the world – using this life for spiritual as well as physical goals.

seeing, not seeing   Most of us see superficially, with the physical body-mind-senses only; mystics speak of inner seeing – *nirat*, the soul's faculty of seeing.

separation, *bireh* The intense pain of separation from the Beloved.

servant, slave   *sévak, daas:* Lover of God, mystic, disciple.

shabd   Lit. word, sound: The divine energy that creates and sustains the universe, audible and visible within everybody as sound and light; also referred to as naam, the name. Recent bhakti mystics have described shabd as the unspoken language, the sound-word (*shabd dhun*) and the sound-based word (*dhunaatmak shabd*), as distinct from *varnaatmak shabd*, words based on letters of an alphabet – differentiating, like Kabir, the eternal word from human words and languages.

Shabd is love itself. When attuned to it inside, it is experienced as blissful, uplifting, magnetic; sometimes described as a personal encounter with an intimate loving being, or being-ness – not merely beautiful music.

shabd form of the master   The master's inner form. Shabd has no form, so the shabd master is formless, beyond subtle bodies and mind. The term is sometimes used for the radiant form.

shabds   Mystics refer to their rhyming compositions as shabds ("words, teachings"), not as poems or poetry.

simran   Remembrance, repetition: Mental repetition of sacred names given by the spiritual teacher to initiates; sometimes referred to as continuous interior prayer.

songpoems   *shabd, pad, ramaini, kunɒli,* etc. The teachings of pre-twentieth century mystics were usually passed on orally in the form of rhyming lyrics – shabds, designed for singing. They were easy for non-readers to memorize, sing and recite, and were composed in the ordinary spoken language of the region so anybody could understand.

sound   *See* **shabd**

surat   In the naam bhakti tradition, surat has several particular meanings: consciousness, soul; also attention and faculty of inner hearing.

surat shabd   A term Kabir and other naam bhakti mystics use for the path and meditation practice they recommend: the merging of surat (consciousness) in shabd (word, sound) at more and more subtle and expanded levels of consciousness.

the thing   *vastu, bastu:* Item, thing; substance, essence, what is real, the real thing. *See also* **naam, shabd**

three worlds   *triloki:* Variously defined by scholars as the trio of the netherworlds, the physical world and the heavens, or the physical, astral and causal levels of consciousness, or the physical (Pind), mental (Brahm) and mental-spiritual (Paar Brahm) levels. However it is defined, triloki falls short of the level of consciousness known as God-realization.

transgressions   *See* **karma**

two, twoness   Duality, multiplicity of forms, illusion of separation and differentiation, *maaya*.

wake up   Awakening of consciousness, spiritual realization.

weeping   *See* **separation**

word   *shabd* in Hindi literally translates as word or sound and refers to ordinary words as well as to the divine power the mystics commonly call the word. *See also* **shabd**

KABIR

It is hard to imagine somebody achieving national fame in their lifetime as poet, mystic and teacher, yet revealing almost nothing about their personal life. But the mystics have always downplayed themselves, insisting that the spiritual teachings are what is important and of lasting value.[1]

So it was with the mystic Kabir. To illustrate something he was teaching, he occasionally mentions his caste or his profession as a weaver; other than that, the focus in his poetry is spirituality, not personality. Bold and outspoken when discussing the mystic philosophy, he records his teachings in hundreds of songpoems and sayings – but gives hardly a line to his own biography.

Stories about the masters, however, have always been told. Passed on from one generation to the next, the stories about Kabir provide us with the few details we know about his life. Most of the "facts" about Kabir, then, are gleaned from oral traditions, scholarly guesswork – and in some cases the knowledge of other mystics.[2]

Kabir was born in medieval times into a poor Muslim weaver's family in Uttar Pradesh, possibly on the outskirts of a small town called Magahar. Tradition holds strong that he died in Magahar and that he lived mostly in Varanasi (Banaras), U.P. – when he was not on the road, travelling to meet disciples all over north and west India.

He earned his living in his family profession as a weaver, supporting his wife and two children – though a few of his poems indicate he sometimes didn't earn enough to keep hunger at bay. Even then, Kabir's humour is not far away.

> Lord, please give me enough
> to contain my family.
> May I not go hungry,
> nor the seekers either![3]

In a poem addressed to the Lord, Kabir reminds him of just what a devotee needs. Kabir uses the word "beg" six times but makes clear that the devotee needs, above all, naam and the company of saints:

> A hungry man can't do his devotions –
> take back this rosary of yours!
> I owe nothing to anyone – but I do beg
> for the dust of the saints' feet.

Sweet Lord, how can I pull on with you?
If you won't give, I'll have to get
by begging: Two kilos of flour, I beg,
and a quarter kilo of ghee and salt.
I beg for half a kilo of lentils –
that should feed me twice a day.[4]

I beg for a cot with four legs,
a pillow and a mattress,
and I beg a quilt for on top.
Then your devotee will worship you
with all his heart most lovingly!

I do not think I've been greedy.
The only thing that is precious to me
is your name. Says Kabir, when my mind
cooperates, when at last it does what I say,
then will I know God.[5]

Oral traditions maintain that Kabir lived to be one
hundred and twenty or so – as did his contemporary,
the mystic Ravidas. No records were kept of births and
deaths in impoverished families, but scholars guess that
Kabir was born at the end of the 1300s and died in the
early 1500s, possibly living from 1398 to 1518.

One of the paradoxes in Kabir's life is that he strongly criticizes all forms of asceticism, ritualistic worship and bigotry, yet according to tradition and an early written record he was initiated by Ramanand, a Hindu ascetic whose practice and lifestyle consisted of everything Kabir denounced.

Why did he seek and accept initiation from such a teacher? Was it to establish a link with a powerful Hindu authority figure in conservative Varanasi? Or was it rather to break through the social barriers so he could directly interact with Ramanand and his disciples?

It was unthinkable in those days for a Brahmin to speak to, look at or initiate someone from a lower caste – let alone a Muslim – so the fact that Kabir managed to get the traditionalist Ramanand to break with convention and initiate him is extraordinary.

According to a manuscript of medieval Hindi songpoems by Ramanand, discovered in Varanasi in the 1930s by PD Badthwal and published in 1955, Ramanand ultimately rejected his own long-held ascetic beliefs (recorded in his Sanskrit treatises, still studied today). This radical change is independently confirmed by a composition of Ramanand's, probably recorded by Nanak in the 1400s, that became part of the Adi Granth in 1604.

In Ramanand's Hindi songpoems he names and praises Kabir as his "true teacher", expressing gratitude to Kabir for initiating him into the path of shabd and waking him up to the delusion of rituals and all external worship.[6]

Fascinating – that a staunch Hindu, a proud and rigid Brahmin like Ramanand, was willing to accept spiritual teachings from a Muslim mystic – a poor weaver who was considered "untouchable" by all his contemporaries. His interactions with Kabir must have convinced him, over time, that Kabir was a mystic of significant power.

Kabir himself repeatedly asserts he is neither Hindu nor Muslim. In one saying he says, for instance:

> If I say I'm a Hindu,
> that's not who I am.
> And I'm not a Muslim either.
>
> Inside this puppet of five elements
> the hidden one
> is at play![7]

He indicates that who we really are – soul, "the hidden one" – has nothing to do with religion, nor even with the body we inhabit. Both are external coverings hiding the essence, soul.

Iconoclast to the last breath, Kabir created quite a stir in his final days. He deliberately left the holy city of Varanasi – where devout Hindus flock to this day in order to die there and be assured of a place in heaven. Aged a hundred and twenty, Kabir walked almost two hundred miles in order to die in infamous Magahar – death there being guaranteed, according to local tradition, to bring about one's rebirth as a donkey!

Kabir probably used the journey as a final opportunity to see disciples along the way – and to convey the message that oneness with the divine has nothing to do with where one dies, but only with how one lives.

In life, at death and ever since, Kabir has been claimed as their own by Muslims and Hindus alike – a reflection of the enormous attraction this mystic had and of his ability to pierce through dogma and prejudice, communicating straight to the heart and mind of his listeners.

Right after Kabir died, an animated discussion took place: should Kabir be cremated like a Hindu or buried like a Muslim? While the Hindu disciples argued their case and the Muslim disciples argued theirs, a few people quietly entered Kabir's hut to sit one last time near the master's body – and found nothing but a fragrant mound of flowers. Those who cared about such things divided the flowers in two: the Muslims buried theirs and the Hindus cremated theirs.

While they may have wept that their master was no longer with them in his physical form, the disciples must have smiled at Kabir's unexpected but characteristic gesture, his final message: Look for me now in a new form! Search for my fragrance, the flower of my being – inside.

Kabir

Says Kabir, I come from a country
with no race or colour, no class or name.
Shabd is what takes you there,
merging you again and again.
Your body? It plays no part
in that merging![8]

KABIR BOOKS

Vigorous language, outspoken assertions and vivid images: these characterize the teaching sayings and songpoems of Kabir, along with gentler inspirational songpoems on love, ecstasy and longing that are perceptive, moving and unusual. While written in a recognizably Kabir style, this entire work on the path of shabd or naam was not actually written down by Kabir himself. He was unable to read or write. So where do all the Kabir "writings" come from?

One early collection, consisting of 228 of Kabir's songpoems and 243 of his sayings, was written down in the 1400s by his contemporary, the Punjabi mystic Nanak, and in the 1500s by Nanak's successors. All of these sayings and songpoems were given a prominent place in the compiling of the Adi Granth in 1604.

In the 1500s, after Kabir's death, a sizeable collection of Kabir's compositions was recorded by the mystic Dadu and his disciple Rajjab in Rajasthan. Dadu had great respect for Kabir and frequently quoted his sayings and songpoems. Rajjab preserved them in *Panch Bani*, a well-known oral anthology of writings from five mystics.

A third collection was written down in Hindi during Kabir's lifetime. Known today as the *Kabir Granthavali*, it was discovered in the 1920s in Varanasi in two separate manuscripts containing a total of 415 songpoems and 940 sayings.

Many Kabir centres, in places he visited, maintained their own written and oral records of Kabir sayings and songpoems – from the *Bijak* in the Varanasi area to collections in far-spread places, including Gujarat with its versions now published as *Kabir Saheb ka Sakhi-Sangrah* and *Satt Kabir ki Shabdavali*.

In the late 1800s the founder of Belvedere Printing Works, Allahabad, and his associates – themselves disciples of a living bhakti teacher – travelled all over north and west India, copying manuscripts and writing down oral traditions of Kabir, Mira, Bullah, Paltu and other bhakti mystics.

Dismissed by scholars because the editors modernized the Hindi spelling, these recordings nevertheless compare favourably with recognized collections that came into print much later on. In the case of Paltu, the Belvedere collection is a primary resource for all other versions.

The Belvedere recordings of Kabir were published from about 1902 on as a series of small volumes – two decades before the discovery of the *Kabir Granthavali*, and many years before standard editions of Kabir's compositions became widely available.

There is now a range of English translations of Kabir, including the following:

+ Selected verses translated by Charlotte Vaudeville (French, 1959; English, 1993)
+ Selected sayings translated by IA Ezekiel (1966)
+ An extensive anthology of mystic songs and sayings translated by VK Sethi (1984)
+ Sayings and songs translated by Linda Hess and Shukdev Singh (sayings 1983, songs 1994)

There are also renderings and translations of Kabir by various poets – for instance:

+ Ezra Pound – Renderings of 10 poems using literal translations by Kali Mohan Ghose (1913)
+ Rabindranath Tagore with Evelyn Underhill – Translations of 100 poems (1915) using a Hindi text and KM Sen's Bengali translation
+ Robert Bly – Renderings of ecstatic poems into contemporary English (1976, 2004) based mainly on the Tagore translation
+ Arvind Krishna Mehrotra – Translations into colloquial American English to evoke Kabir's style (2011)

Wake up! if you can (2015) is a selection of 101 sayings of Kabir with reflections and mystic stories. New translations from the Hindi, the sayings focus on love and longing with glimpses of ecstasy and the transformation process Kabir calls *surat shabd* – the merging of consciousness (surat) in shabd, the word.

ENDNOTES

Originals: A transliteration of the Hindi has been provided throughout the book for the convenience of Hindi speakers – and for those who don't understand Hindi but want a sense of what Kabir's sayings sound like and what their rhythm feels like.

Sounds: In earlier times, the same letter was used for "s" and "sh" – so *shareer* and *shabd*, for instance, are pronounced "sh" but were written *sareer* and *sabd*. Shabd ("*a*" as in uh-huh) is pronounced *shabd* in Hindi and *shabad* in Punjabi and many dialects. Retroflex sounds, pronounced at the back of the mouth, are indicated with small caps: *ja ghaт pargaт hoé*. The nasal sound is indicated with a ~ tilde: *téra saaee~ tujjh mé~*.

Structure: In Hindi the first line of a Kabir saying or *doha* usually sets up an image or proposition; the second line responds to it with something of a bang. The rhythm is brisk, the lines short – and Kabir makes every word count, omitting whatever is not essential for impact and meaning.

This book is an enlarged edition of the original Pocketbook version by the same title (2014). A few of the translations were first published in *The inner way: A mystic anthology of songpoems, stories, reflections* (Salt River Publishing, 2013).

Introduction

1. Juan de la Cruz lived in Spain in the 1500s at the time of the Spanish Inquisition. As a Barefoot Carmelite reformer working with Teresa of Avila, he was imprisoned twice by the orthodox Carmelite authorities. And as an unorthodox thinker, a mystic, his life was always at risk from the convenors of the Inquisition.

   Cf. Gerald Brenan, *Saint John of the Cross: his life and poetry* (Cambridge University Press, 1975).

2. HINDI SAYING, GHAT MATH SECTION
   jyo~ til maahee~ tél hai, jyo~ chakmak mé~ aag;
   téra saaee~ tujjh mé~, jaagi saké to jaagi.

3. HINDI SAYING, SHABD SECTION
   sabad baraabar dhan nahee~, jo koé jaanai bol;
   heera to daamo~ milai, sabadahi~ bol na tol.

4. HINDI SAYING, NAAM SECTION
   koti naam sa~saar mé~, ta té~ mukti na hoé;
   aadi naam jo gupt jap, boojhai birla koé.

   The primal or *aadi* name means it existed before the creation began – beyond time, body, mind and languages: a power or energy, not a name in the common sense of the term. *boojhai* in the last line, "realize", refers to spiritual transformation and enlightenment as well as intellectual understanding.

5. HINDI SHABDAVALI, CHITAAVANI AUR UPDÉSH, EXCERPT from *"adhar hi ruyaal"*:

*sabd ghanghor ᴛᴀnkor taha~ adhar hai, noor ko parasi
ké peer paaya;*
*kaihai kabeer yaha khél avadhoot ka, khéli avadhoot ghar
saihaij aaya.*

6. The real form of the bhakti master is shabd, not the
physical body. Although one can see him physically, his
shabd form is in Gagan, the "skies" of consciousness. By
the same token, the real form of a disciple is *chit* (line
1) or *surat* (line 2): consciousness – not body or mind,
but soul. See also SAYING 27 and endnote.

HINDI SAYING, GURUDÉV SECTION
guru hamaara gagan mé~, chéla hai chit maahi~;
surat sabad méla bhaya, bichhuʀat kabahoo~ naahi~.

7. "The word became flesh and made its dwelling among
us, full of grace and truth" (New Testament, *John* 1:14).

8. If the master and God are one, why does anybody need
a master in human form – why not worship God direct?
Kabir pinpoints here what prevents us from doing so:
ego, the mind.

HINDI SAYING, GURUDÉV SECTION
guru saahib to ék hai~, dooja sab aakaar;
aapa méᴛé guru bhajé, tab paavai kartaar.

9. *balihaari* lit. means sacrifice; here it conveys the warrior
disciple's joyful and triumphant submission of self. The
master "tells about God" – he teaches and makes possible

the practice that leads to the state of consciousness where God and guru are both seen "standing here". God is always here, but the master is essential for realizing his presence.

HINDI SAYING, GURUDÉV SECTION
guru gobind do'oo khaʀé, ka ké laagau~ paa~é;
balihaari guru aapané, jin gobind diyo bataaé.

10. Disciples may think they make great efforts and sacrifices to follow the path – they do, but Kabir's point is: What motivates them to do all this? It is the Lord himself, pulling from inside. And he adds: Unless the Lord comes as a master, how would the yearning of seekers and disciples ever be fulfilled?

HINDI SAYING, GURUDÉV SECTION
paihilé daata sish bhaya, jin tan man arpa sees;
paachhé daata guru bhayé, jin naam diya baksees.

11. Kabir mentions wedding bed, a sideways reminder that the soul's wedding night and union with the Beloved take place right inside these bodies of clay – by raising our consciousness to where the Beloved manifests inside. Kabir says "I am a sacrifice" to people like that – a strong expression of blessings and appreciation for what those disciples have accomplished.

HINDI SAYING, SÉVAK AUR DAAS SECTION
sab ghaт méra saa'iyaa~, sooni séj na koé;
balihaari va ghaтт ki, ja ghaт pargaт hoé.

For more on *ghaṭ*, "clay pot, body of clay", used three times here, see endnote on SAYING 19.

12. Cf. *Shams-e Tabrizi* (SSRC, 2011), pp.20-21, 206-207.

13. For comments on this *doha*, see SAYING 7, p.26.

14. With thanks to RB for the Hindi.
    HINDI SAYING, COMMONS
    kabeer man nirmal bhaya, jaisé ganga neer;
    paachhé paachhé hari phirai, kaihait kabeer kabeer.

Sayings

1. SAYING 4 One mystic speaks of the fragrance of compassion, kindness, forgiveness, sweetness of language, helpfulness to others – the kind of fragrance, one might add, that is obvious in the masters.

2. SAYING 5 See Glossary for information on karma. Heart: eye centre. Debts: *paap*, sins.

3. SAYING 7 In another poem on the *bhédi*/diviner theme, Kabir implies that we have spent years, lifetimes, searching unsuccessfully for realization:

   The thing is one place, you're searching someplace else – how do you expect to find it?
   Says Kabir, you'll only get it when you take the diviner along: he knows the secret.

bastu kahee~ ᴅᴏᴏ~ᴅai kahee~, kéhi bidhi aavai haath;
kaihai kabeer tab paa'iyé, jab bhédi leejé saath.

4. SAYING 9 As human beings, our soul is a leaf on the tree
   of the divine. Unlike animals, we have discrimination:
   we know right from wrong. When this life is over,
   depending on our actions we may or may not "fall off
   the tree". If the soul does fall, we go down into the vast
   cycle of transmigration. As a carrot or cockroach, we lose
   our potential for God-realization – we cannot "rejoin
   the tree". So the present life is precious, not to be wasted.

   To get really technical: Kabir's leaf/tree image may refer
   to the karmic law of *karm jooni* and *bhog jooni*. The
   soul in a human body undergoes old karma and creates
   new karma. It is *karm jooni* – responsible for facing
   the consequences, at some point, of all its actions from
   this life. But as a human, the soul also has the unique
   potential to spiritually realize its oneness with God.

   Souls in the lower species, on the other hand, create no
   karma at all. They passively undergo – *bhog jooni* – the
   results of actions done in previous lives as humans. Their
   freedom from responsibility for karma is balanced by
   their inability to "join the tree": they cannot become
   God-realized in that life or series of lives in the lower
   species.

5. SAYING 10 Kabir appeals to the great nostalgia within each person. That love is what will keep the lover awake at night, meditating – longing to see.

6. SAYING 11 Soul's hearing and seeing: *surat* and *nirat*, the inner faculties of soul consciousness.

7. SOURCE OF THE STORIES IN THIS BOOK: Commons – tales from various traditions, told by mystics.

8. SAYING 13 HINDI: Commons.

9. SAYING 16 For a discussion of *ghaT*, body, see endnote, SAYING 19.

10. SAYING 17 Unhappiness, worry, grief, fear, etc. are associated with attention below the eye centre.

11. SAYING 19 In the sayings Kabir uses a variety of words for body, including *ghaT/ghaaT* (clay pot), *sareer, déh, tan* (often paired with *man*, mind). Most of the time the expression *ghaT mé~* (inside the clay pot) translates adequately as inside, inside yourself, deep inside you. But occasionally *ghaT* is a subtle reminder that this temporary everyday ordinary-looking disposable clay pot of a body is a container for something far more significant: the water of life, shabd.

12. SAYING 20 *ramna* lit. means to roam around, enjoy oneself. So shabd roams around enjoying itself inside everything?

13. SAYING 21 The Hindi word *shabd* literally means sound, word.

14. SAYING 22 In modern Hindi the verb *gaihaina* means to seize, take hold of; it literally means to thresh.

15. SAYING 23 In another saying Kabir addresses people who are obsessed with their looks:

    > Better to be meditating on the name and dying
    > of AIDS, pus oozing from your sores. What's
    > the point of a golden body if you don't have
    > the name in your mouth?

    HINDI SAYING, NAAM SECTION
    naam japat kushᴛhi bhalaa, chu'i chu'i parai jo chaam;
    ka~chan déh kéhi kaam ki, ja mukh naahee~ naam.
    kushᴛhi, lit. leper.

16. SAYING 25 For soul to be liberated (*oobarai*) it needs to somehow be pulled beyond the worlds governed by mind, karma and transmigration. It cannot go there of its own volition, through its own power and energy.

17. STORY OF THE SIEVE Based on Trevor Leggett, *Encounters in Yoga and Zen: Meetings of Cloth and Stone* (1983), a collection of traditional Japanese and Indian stories used in some mystic schools for training seekers and practitioners.

18. SAYING 27 Technically the upper reaches of the worlds governed by the universal mind are called Gagan ("the sky of mind"). Pure sound devoid of mind: i.e., shabd of Sunn, the Void, beyond mind, karma and transmigration.

19. SAYING 28 Finding a satguru outside leads to seeing the light and the radiant form of the master inside.

20. SAYING 31 When the attention is brought to a complete focus inside, one becomes unconscious of the body. This temporary withdrawal is referred to by mystics as dying while living, dying while alive, dying before death, dying daily. The home of love: the highest level of consciousness, full realization.

21. SAYING 34 *mil*, find, meet, merge (used in the first and second lines) is the root of *milan*, the meeting of bride and groom, marital union. See also SAYINGS 22, 28, 47, 51, 62 and endnote, SAYING 51. *amrit* (nectar) means deathless, immortal – a drink that gives eternal life.

22. SAYING 35 *doha* thanks to VK Sethi, noted 1982; HINDI SOURCE untraced at the time of going to press.

23. SAYING 37 Mystics often describe the master as a washerman (*dhobi*) or dyer (*rang-réz*) who cleans the mind. Being dyed by the satguru in the colour of naam dissolves the mind's expectations and desires, imbuing it permanently with God's love. Thanks to RB for her inputs on *bairaag*, detachment, in line 1.

24. SAYING 38 Any name: lit. Motiya, "little pearl". Moti is so commonly used for pet dogs in India that one doesn't think of its real meaning – or its root: *mukti*, liberation. i.e., The servant disciple is spiritually realized!

25. SAYING 42 In the karmic scheme of things, devotion earns a karmic reward – but to reap that reward we have to be reborn. So we go on interacting, desiring and creating more karmic debts… The solution? To follow the master beyond the mind to full realization of God.

    Humour and forcefulness are built into the Hindi by Kabir's repetition of the same sounds and phrases used wittily and unexpectedly – in particular *hari…jani* in line 1 (don't love God), a play on *harijan* in lines 1 and 2 (God's people – his lovers or devotees), the masters, who give one thing only: *harihee~*, God, only God.

26. SAYING 45 Blue moon rain: lit. rain during the constellation of Swati or Swaanti. Folklore says that a pearl is formed when a drop of Swaanti rain falls inside an oyster shell. See also endnote, SAYING 65.

27. SAYING 51 The verb *milana* (meet, mix, merge, join), much used by mystics and easy to miss, conveys various associations of lover/beloved. For instance, *milan* is the meeting of bride and groom – marital union. So "when is he coming to meet me" in Hindi reverberates more intimately than in English. See also endnote SAYING 34.

28. AYAAZ STORY At least two of the Ayaaz stories were told by Shams of Tabriz (1100s), just one hundred years after Ayaaz. Cf. Farida Maleki, *Shams-e Tabrizi: Rumi's perfect teacher* (SSRC, 2011), pp.190-192, 216.

29. SAYING 56 *guru charan*, the master's lotus feet, connotes the inner form of the master, the radiant form – and his constant presence. See also endnote, SAYING 60.

30. SAYING 57 "Marked souls" sounds like a Christian concept, but in fact all mystics speak of the particular souls they have been sent to collect (initiate, guide home), casually referred to here by Kabir with the word "introduction". My thanks to HG for help tying this saying together.

31. SAYING 58 HINDI SOURCE untraced at the time of going to press.

32. IDEAL DISCIPLE STORY Kabir's analogies recall his dec-ades of travelling on foot all over north and west India.

33. SAYING 60 Total surrender of self to the lotus feet, *charan ka~val*, refers to communion, oneness, with the radiant form of the master. See also endnote, SAYING 56.

34. SAYING 62 In India the call of the rainbird is *piu piu* ("beloved, beloved"). *milan*: see endnotes, SAYINGS 34, 51.

35. SAYING 63 The images in this saying are open to several interpretations, including: The soul (fish) cannot survive

if deprived of the water of spirituality, nor can we survive underneath the waters of the world.

36. SAYING 65 Blue moon rain: see endnote, SAYING 45. Pearl, *moti*, has the same root as *mukti*, liberation.

37. SAYING 69 *laal, laalee* – red, redness, ruby, son, darling – is used five times in this saying and doesn't have an obvious equivalent in English. Taking a look at his radiance means seeing the radiant or inner light form of the master, merging in shabd. The last line is in the feminine (*ga'i, ho ga'i*): the lover is a woman in relation to the Beloved.

38. SAYING 74 All fears and worries, including the fear of the unknown (death, dying and what happens after death), leave us only when we go beyond the mind.

39. SAYING 80 Rituals in different traditions include a special drink – hemp, amrit, wine or grape juice, for example – that is said to bestow spiritual benefit. For Kabir, the real immortalizing drink is naam, shabd.

    Repetition of the same words with multiple meanings in the Hindi intensifies the tone of love and intoxication in this saying.

40. SAYING 81 Phaagun, the context of the poem, is the month in spring when Holi, the joyful and passionate festival of colours, is celebrated. Repetition, echoing sounds and multiple meanings intensify the feeling of

intoxication in the Hindi, emphasizing two key words: *roop* (form, beauty, face, figure, elegance, grace, etc.) and *rang* (colour, beauty, pleasure, joy, love, etc.).

EXCERPT from *ritu phaagun niyaraani*.

41. SAYING 82 Orgy: *saakat* is lit. a worshipper of Shakti – associated in medieval times with practices that involved sex, alcohol, drugs, animal sacrifice, blood rituals and human sacrifice.

42. SAYING 84 Nobody volunteers to burn down their own house – but when the fire is passion for the divine and the house is our ego, it begins to make sense. The five passions, when conquered, are sometimes referred to as five small boys. Absorption in naam goes along with overcoming the passions and the mind; the one requires the other.

    In the last line Kabir plays with two meanings of *lau*: to be absorbed in (naam) and to be set on fire by (naam) – neatly linking the first and last lines.

43. SAYING 85 Kabir's Hindi leaves the last line a tad ambiguous – on purpose? At first it looks like a clear reference to Kabir being pulled out; but it could also be interpreted as Kabir doing the pulling. Once committed to the inward way, we will know who is drifting – and who is capable of rescuing us.

44. SAYING 87 Divine love and passion for the Beloved is what creates detachment from everything else – "house"

or ego-self and personal identity – putting an end to our sense of separateness from the Beloved. VK Sethi in 1982 pointed out that in some versions of this widespread saying, the word for torch is *ramaada,* a reed torch used for lighting a funeral pyre!

45. SAYING 89 In another saying on sleep, Kabir says:

> Sleep when you're awake. Be absorbed when you're asleep. Keep your attention tied to the DOR, the cord, current or stream. Then the *taar,* the strings or music, will never break.

With attention absorbed in the sound current inside, the music remains unbroken. Shabd is then heard continuously, all day, all night: the real way to be "asleep when awake", unaffected by the world.

HINDI SAYING, NIDRA SECTION
jaagan mé~ sovan karai, sovan mé~ lau laaé;
surati DOR laagi rahai, taar TOOTI nahi~ jaaé.

46. SAYING 91 The negative qualities of the mind prevent one from consistently experiencing selfless love. Kabir says: overcome ego (name, family, colour) – then you'll be capable of devotion.

47. SAYING 92 The word *bishTa* in the last line lit. means human feces – not something as acceptable as dirt, filth, dung or manure – causing early twentieth-century editors to cringe at Kabir's crude language. Kabir lived

at a time in India and many other places when people of the working class, known until recently in India as untouchables, were literally treated like shit. As an "untouchable" himself, Kabir knew what it was like. In this poem he names it.

48. NASRUDDIN STORY Back in the 1950s and 60s, Idries Shah told, wrote and published versions of the "Mulla Nasrudin" stories in English, making them well known in Europe and North America.

49. SAYING 94 "Truth" is a common mystic term for the eternal and unchanging divine essence (shabd, naam).

50. SAYING 95 The nineteenth-century mystic Shiv Dayal Singh of Agra classifies spoken/written words as *varnaatmak shabd* or descriptive, alphabet-based, letter-based words; the eternal divine power or word of God, he calls *dhunaatmak shabd* or sound-based word.

51. SAYING 96 Alchemy has been used as a metaphor for hundreds of years to convey mystic transformation. The philosopher is the master; the philosophers' stone is naam; turning base metal into gold is the transformation of the mind so it emerges in its highest, priceless form.

52. ROSE PETAL STORY Kabir and Nanak were contemporaries. Some say Nanak was a disciple of Kabir – one of his spiritual successors. Besides Nanak, other possible Kabir successors include Ravidas of Varanasi and

Rajasthan; and Kabir's disciple Dharm Das of Varanasi. A large number of Kabir's sayings and songpoems were written down by Nanak (1400s) and given remarkable prominence in the Adi Granth, the spiritual anthology compiled in 1604 by Arjan, fifth master in the line of Nanak. The Adi Granth also includes verses of Ravidas and other mystics.

53. SAYING 97 In this well-known saying of Kabir's, he refers to the extraordinary power of the saint's company. Are sinners transformed into saints overnight? It has happened – but generally the mystics say the impact of seeing or spending time in the satsang of a master is that sooner or later, in this life or a future life, the soul is given an opportunity to follow the inner path.

54. SAYING 98 Last line: "That's how I became Kabir (the teacher/mystic)" or "That's how I became *kabeer* (the Great One)" – *kabeer* being a name for God in the Qur'an. Either way, Kabir gives the credit to his lord and master and to God – *saahib* in the last line lit. meaning owner, associate, companion, master, lord, God.

55. SAYING 99 Once, we were unable to bear the shabd – that lake of bliss. But this changes as body and mind are strengthened and purified – through the inner practice, daily dipping into shabd. The birds of attachments, desires and sense pleasures no longer receive the water of the world: we have begun to drink a different water.

56. SAYING 100 "Attachment creates detachment" might be Kabir but isn't – it's a contemporary mystic, summing up the mystic way in a nutshell.

Kabir bio

1. Even today, in their talks and writings, contemporary mystics give little personal information. As one mystic says, *The master's biography is his disciples.* Disciples "write" the story of the master's life by the way they put into practice his teachings.

2. For insights on Kabir and his life, see books like VK Sethi's *Kabir, the Weaver of God's Name* (RSSB, 1984), the Sant Bani Ashram's *Ocean of Love: the Anurag Sagar of Kabir*, pp.xvii–xxvi (1982), Linda Hess and Shukdev Singh's *Bijak* (1983) and Robert Bly's *Winged Energy of Delight*, pp.37–55 (2005).

3. "Seekers": *saadh*, lit. renunciants, mendicants, sadhus – the spiritual seekers of all types who would visit Kabir.

   KABIR SAYING, VISHVAAS SECTION
   saaee~ itna deejié, ja me~ kuᴛumb samaay; mai~ bhee bhookha na rahoo~, saadhu na bhookha jaay.

4. This should keep me fed twice a day: Kabir proposes, tongue-in-cheek, that the devotee needs this much food indefinitely for two square meals a day in order to be fit for devotions!

5. **KABIR, ADI GRANTH, RAAG SORATH, p.656:11:1–4.**

   1: *bhookhé bhagati na keejai, yaha maala apanee leejai;*
   ham maangau santan réna, mai nahee kisee ka déna.

   maadho kaisee banai tum sangé, aapi na déhu ta lévaho
   mangé (rahaao).

   2: *du'i sér maangao choona, paao gheeo sangi loona;*
   adh séru maangao daalé, mo kao donao vakhat jivaalé.

   3: *khaaт maangao chaopaaee, sirhaana avar tulaaee;*
   oopar kao maangao kheendha, téri bhagati karai janu
   theendha.

   4: *mai naahee keeta labo, iku naao téra mai phabo;*
   kahi kabeer manu maania, man maania tao hari jaania.

6. *Ramanand ki hindi rachnae,* ed. PD Badthwal (Varanasi, 1955).

7. **HINDI SAYING, MADHYA SECTION**
   hindoo kahoo~ to mai~ nahee~, musalmaan bhee naahi~;
   paa~ch tatva ka pootala, gaibi khélai maahi~.

8. The process of merging in shabd is not a one-time experience. Repeated over and over (*sabd milaava hoé raha*), it ultimately merges soul in the source of shabd: the supreme being – the land of Kabir.

   HINDI SAYING, PARICHAY SECTION
   ham baasi us dés ké, jaha~ jaati baran kul naahi~;
   sabd milaava hoé raha, déh milaava naahi~.

INDEX OF SAYINGS

A few of the sayings were first published in the *Inner Way* anthology (Salt River Publishing, 2013), reprinted here with permission and referred to as *IW*.

SALT RIVER

Salt River Publishing believes in encouraging artists and publishing professionals to come together and reach their empowered "Yes!"

Salt River was established as a no-profit publisher to help writers, translators, poets, graphic artists and photographers bring their work into publishable form and make 100% of the profit on their book sales.

And to promote, for free, the expertise of publishing professionals whose services an author might need when they have a book in the making.

We publish books that inspire, encourage or entertain, including children's books – and books that deepen the understanding of mysticism.

Do you have one?

www.SaltRiverPublishing.com

READER RESPONSE
TO SALT RIVER BOOKS

"So many problems are spiritual in nature. And healing often involves finding meaning, purpose and spiritual uplift. The right words at the right time can turn a life around. Therapists and practitioners can point the way for clients who are seeking meaning; writers and artists have an opportunity to share in that work. Thank you, Salt River."

INDEX OF STORIES

ACKNOWLEDGEMENTS

As always, I feel deep gratitude for my teachers – and for supportive friends, family and colleagues. It is a pleasure to acknowledge a few by name; I thank also the ones not named here.

Much appreciation to both my sisters: Chloe Faith Wordsworth, for her significant suggestions, feedback – and stories; and Lindis Guinness, for her feedback on presentation and content.

And to Faith Singh, whose bhakti assignment in 2010 unexpectedly morphed into the Salt River books.

The commentary in this book is a team effort. Many thanks to the four colleagues who helped me transform the original versions.

In the first POCKETBOOK edition: Appreciation to Berkeley Digby; Cindy Rawlinson, Connie Rawlinson, Melanie Vogel, Margaret Humbert-Droz and Barbara Maynord; and to the readers who asked for more – which resulted in this expanded edition.

To Renu Bhagat for carefully reviewing the translations; to Honey Girdhar for happily addressing the odd Hindi question; and to the colleagues who tracked down elusive *dohas*. The errors are mine.

To Carol White, designer of books, for collaborating, as always. And to Greg Meyer for the cover photo.

Special thanks to Robert Bly for *The Eight Stages of Translation* – a marvellous guide for any translator of poetry.

And to VK Sethi, author of *Kabir, the weaver of God's Name* and *Mira, the divine lover*. Colleague, mentor, friend, he shared his love for Kabir and years ago filled my mind with images of India's traditions – secular, literary and spiritual – that I've been drawing on ever since.

Profound gratitude for my family! My parents, John and Karis Guinness – their love, positive support and open-minded approach to all religions paved the way for everything that has followed; my grandparents, especially Grace and Geraldine, all born in the 1800s – pioneers in their own generation who rose above limitations and convention in pursuit of their dreams; and my two sisters, Lindis and Chloe – special appreciation for all their love, and for lifelong friendship, encouragement, shared interests, and so many good memories…

Acknowledgements

Wake up! if you can gives a tiny hint of the extraordinary nature of true spiritual teachers. Gratitude to my master and his successor cannot be expressed in words… The masters say "Love needs to be packaged as meditation", so may the grace of daily effort remain to our very last breath!

EDITOR/TRANSLATOR

In 1975 Anthea Guinness went to India on a 9-month Hindi scholarship and stayed for twenty-nine years. She studied, taught, translated – and copy-edited books on the bhakti tradition. With a PhD in comparative religion, she is the founder of Salt River Publishing and lives now in Arizona.

APPRECIATION

$\mathcal{T}$hank you

for buying a copy of this book.

Available at Amazon.com
and
SaltRiverPublishing.com
Discount available at the SRP estore

SALT RIVER BOOKLIST

Global Library Books
+ Janice Fletcher, EdD – *Teach with Spirit: A teacher's inward journey guide*
+ Anthea Guinness – *The inner way: A mystic anthology of songpoems, stories, reflections*   SUITABLE FOR AGE 13 ON UP
+ Anthea Guinness – *Wake up! if you can: Sayings of Kabir with reflections and mystic stories*
+ Anthea Guinness – *Soami Ji of Agra answering questions: Mystic teachings on the path of inner sound*, 2 vols.

Tuppany Books
+ Shanan Harrell – *Stumbling towards enlightenment* *K
+ Rosemary Rawson – *Coming of age* *K
+ Elley-Ray Tsipolitis – *Butterfly kisses*

Pocketbooks
+ Anthea Guinness – *Dawn has come: Songpoems of Paltu*

*K for KINDLE

Beyond Borders Books
- Dyan Dubois – *Rajasthan suite memory* (*a novel*) *K

New Moon Books for children
- Tia Pleiman, Village Voices series – *I am the rainbow, With my hands, Color in the book, In my dreams*

Eye of an Artist Books
- Greg Meyer – *Arizona places: Otherworldly and beautiful*

Independent Publications *Salt River assistance with editing, book design, composition, cover design*
- Rosemary Rawson – ***Dark bread and dancing***
- Chloe Faith Wordsworth – ***Quantum change, Spiral up!*** and eleven other Resonance Repatterning books

www.SaltRiverPublishing.com

COLOPHON

Typefaces: Adobe Brioso Pro (designed by Robert Slimbach), Vatican (designed by Alan Meeks), Adobe Jensen Pro (designed by Nicolas Jensen and Robert Slimbach)
Software: Adobe InDesign
Book Design: Anthea Guinness and Carol White
Composition: Anthea Guinness
Cover Photo, used with permission: Greg Meyer MD, MD(H) – meyerhomeopathy.com
Cover Design: Carol White of Salt River Publishing – *email*: carol@saltriverpublishing.com
Printer: createspace.com
Printing method: Print-on-Demand (POD) digital printing
Paper: Library quality
Binding: Perfect binding

www.SaltRiverPublishing.com